Ecclesiastes

A Document Designed to Disturb

Coy D. Roper

CYPRESS

Copyright © 2022

Manufactured in the United States

Cataloging-in-Publication Data

Roper, Coy D. (Coy Dee).

Ecclesiastes: a document designed to disturb / by Coy D. Roper

p. cm.

Includes Scripture index.

ISBN: 978-1-956811-23-0 (pbk.); 978-1-956811-24-7 (ebook)

1. Bible. Ecclesiastes—Study and teaching. 2. Bible. Ecclesiastes—Criticism, interpretation, etc. I. Author. II. Title.

223.806—dc20

Library of Congress Control Number: 2022907335

Cover design by Brad McKinnon and Brittany Vander Maas.

For information:

Cypress Publications
3625 Helton Drive
PO Box HCU
Florence, AL 35630

www.hcu.edu

Contents

Bible Abbreviations

Old Testament

Gen	Genesis
Exod	Exodus
Lev	Leviticus
Num	Numbers
Deut	Deuteronomy
Josh	Joshua
Judg	Judges
Ruth	Ruth
1–2 Sam	1–2 Samuel
1–2 Kgs	1–2 Kings
1–2 Chr	1–2 Chronicles
Ezra	Ezra
Neh	Nehemiah
Esth	Esther
Job	Job

Ps	Psalms
Prov	Proverbs
Eccl	Ecclesiastes
Song	Song of Solomon
Isa	Isaiah
Jer	Jeremiah
Lam	Lamentations
Ezek	Ezekiel
Dan	Daniel
Hos	Hosea
Joel	Joel
Amos	Amos
Obad	Obadiah
Jonah	Jonah
Mic	Micah
Nah	Nahum
Hab	Habakkuk
Zeph	Zephaniah
Hag	Haggai
Zech	Zechariah
Mal	Malachi

New Testament

Matt	Matthew
Mark	Mark
Luke	Luke
John	John
Acts	Acts

Rom	Romans
1–2 Cor	1–2 Corinthians
Gal	Galatians
Eph	Ephesians
Phil	Philippians
Col	Colossians
1–2 Thess	1–2 Thessalonians
1–2 Tim	1–2 Timothy
Titus	Titus
Phlm	Philemon
Heb	Hebrews
Jas	James
1–2 Pet	1–2 Peter
1–2–3 John	1–2–3 John
Jude	Jude
Rev	Revelation

1. An Introduction to the Book of Ecclesiastes[1]

W hen you read the Bible, you should come away from your reading feeling comforted, feeling good, feeling happy. Right? Most of the time. But we want to begin a study of a book that was meant to make you uncomfortable. That book is Ecclesiastes. In this lesson we want to introduce the book, consider its contents briefly, and think about how it should be interpreted.

Introduction: Classification, Author, Title, Purpose[2]

Classification. In the English Old Testament, Ecclesiastes is classified as one of the Books of Poetry, in spite of the fact that (unlike Job, Psalms, Proverbs, and Song of Solomon) it is written mostly in prose.

In the Hebrew Bible, Ecclesiastes is classified as one

of the books of the Writings. Within that category, it is placed (along with Ruth, Esther, Lamentations, and Song of Solomon) among the five little books called the *Megilloth* which were read at various feasts of the Jews. Ecclesiastes was read at the Feast of Tabernacles.

Ecclesiastes is also classified, along with Job and Proverbs, as one of the books of Wisdom Literature. One reason it deserves this designation is that it emphasizes wisdom. The words "wisdom" or "wise" or "wisely" are found about fifty times in the book, and its opposite—"foolishness," or "fool," or "folly"—is found about twenty-eight times in the text (in the two-hundred-twenty-one verses of Ecclesiastes).

The wisdom tradition in Israel can be divided into two kinds of literature, called by some:

1. "Optimistic"—exemplified by Proverbs (which seems to say, for the most part, that God rewards the righteous with prosperity).
2. "Pessimistic"—exemplified by Job (which asks why the righteous suffer) and Ecclesiastes (which questions whether anything one does in this life makes any difference anyway).

Author. According to tradition in both Judaism and Christianity, the author was Solomon. Tradition says that Solomon wrote three books:

1. *Song of Solomon*, when he was young.
2. *Proverbs*, when he was middle-aged.
3. *Ecclesiastes*, when he was old.

The author, although he does not name himself, sounds like Solomon, or like someone very much like Solomon. He calls himself "the son of David, king in Jerusalem" (1:1); he says he was "king over Israel in Jerusalem" (1:12); and he speaks of his achievements, wisdom, and riches (2:3–8)—all characteristics of King Solomon (see 1 Kgs 3, 4).

Questions have been raised about whether Solomon was really the author of Ecclesiastes because the author does not call himself Solomon and some of the things he says sound strange coming from a king. In addition, Solomon lived in the tenth century B.C. and some scholars think that the style and vocabulary of the writing point to a later date, to the fourth or third century B.C. Also, some scholars think that the highly developed wisdom movement evidenced by the book occurred at a date considerably later than Solomon's time.

Probably the best course for us to take is to accept the words of the text as literal, and therefore to accept Solomon as the author. (If it was not Solomon, then it was someone writing who put himself in the place of Solomon and wrote as if he were Solomon.)   Most important: we believe that, whoever the human author was, the book was inspired by God.

Title. The title "Ecclesiastes" comes from the Septuagint[3] translation of the Hebrew title and means "The Preacher." In English the book begins: "The words of the Preacher ..." (1:1). The Hebrew name for the book is *Qoheleth*, the first word of the text. *Qoheleth* is derived from a Hebrew verb which means "to assemble." The idea may be "leader of the assembly" or "one who speaks before the assembly."

Purpose. The author himself explains the reason why he wrote the book and why he chose to write in the style he used. First, he intended to "seek and explore ... concerning all that has been done under heaven" (1:12). He made a systematic effort to discover a universal explanation for everything (he said he had applied his "mind to every deed that has been done under the sun" [8:9]). He succeeded in his quest to learn, saying, "All this I came to see as wisdom under the sun, and it impressed me" (9:13). Consequently, having considered everything and learned much, the author fulfilled his purpose by teaching what he had learned to others: "The Preacher also taught the people knowledge" (12:9). And he did so by using the best means of communication available: "many proverbs" and "delightful words" used correctly (12:9, 10).

The author's purpose was, therefore, threefold:

1. to learn the truth about everything and so to discover the meaning of life,
2. to teach others that truth, and
3. to use the best words possible to communicate the truth that he had learned.

Contents

The theme of the book—announced in Ecclesiastes 1:2 and repeated over and over again—is "Vanity:" "'Vanity of vanities,' says the Preacher, 'Vanity of vanities! All is vanity.'"[4] The message is that life is vain ... empty ... meaningless.

The author's concern therefore is to try to find and communicate the meaning of life. In effect, he asks: Although it appears that all is vain, is there anything that gives life meaning? He explores a number of man's activities and concludes that, no, these do not make life meaningful.

Understood in the author's discussion is the fact that what is under consideration is life "under the sun" (a phrase found fifteen times in fourteen verses)[5]—life experienced by man, life on this earth, leaving God out of consideration—is meaningless.

However, the author says, since we are destined to spend our life on this earth "under the sun,"[6] we need to live in the best way possible. That way could be summed up as the way of wisdom. While wisdom alone will not altogether solve the problems that make life meaningless (the problem of death, for instance), and while wisdom can itself be overrated, the person who lives wisely will enjoy a much better life "under the sun." Living wisely includes acquiring knowledge, but is not limited to the acquisition of knowledge. Wisdom is the application of knowledge; among other things, the wise person will live happily with his or her spouse, and he or she will enjoy life and avoid the mistakes which fools make which ruin their lives. This is man's lot—this is what man should do during his brief stay on this earth "under the sun."

But in the end, in view of the coming of death, of judgment, and of eternity, there is really only one thing that makes human life truly meaningful--and that is to serve God acceptably. This is the single major idea that the writer of Ecclesiastes is striving to get across, the conclusion towards which the whole book moves. The book ends with these words: "The conclusion, when all has been said, is: fear God and keep His command-ments, because this applies to every person. For God will bring every act to judgment, everything which is hidden, whether it is good or evil" (Eccl 12:13, 14, NASB; more familiar are the words of the KJV: "for this is the whole duty of man").

Interpretation

Like the other books classified as "wisdom literature," Ecclesiastes includes sayings which may sound strange to our ears, if, in reading it, we expect to hear the will of God expressed in commands to us. Some things we read in this book may even cause us to pause and shake our heads and say to ourselves, "that is not so," or, "that is not always true or not altogether true."

For example, consider the following statements from the book:

"There is an appointed time for everything ... . A time to love and a time to hate ... " (3:1, 8). Should we ever hate?

"I have seen that nothing is better than that man should be happy in his activities" (3:22). Is not doing God's will better, regardless of whether it makes us happy or not?

Concerning the "sons of men:" "God has surely tested them in order for them to see that they are but beasts" (4:18). Are human beings nothing but "beasts"?

"The day of one's death is better than the day of one's birth" (7:1). Is that really true, or always true?

"Do not be excessively righteous and do not be overly wise" (7:16). How is it possible to be too righteous or too wise?

How should one interpret such passages as these?

Wisdom literature is not law. The books of wisdom,

though they may restate the law and reflect the law and apply the law, are not books of law. The law of God is unbending, always true, never to be broken. "Thou shalt not commit adultery" means what it says and says what it means. But the Old Testament contains other types of literature; not every statement should be interpreted as if it were an unbreakable law.

When should what the writer of Ecclesiastes says be interpreted as if it were law? When it restates or elaborates on one of the laws of the Mosaic system. That statement in Ecclesiastes then becomes "law," but only because it repeats a law found elsewhere.

Writers use figurative language. The authors of the wisdom books (as of other Old Testament books) often use figures of speech—similes, metaphors, hyperbole, etc. To understand what the writer was intending to say, one needs to recognize that he may be using figurative language. To interpret a figure of speech as if it were meant to be understood literally is to misinterpret what the author was saying.

For example, imagine that your buddy George says of another friend of yours, "Johnny is a chicken." Would you respond, "No, he's not. He doesn't have wings or feathers, and I've never heard him cluck or seen him lay an egg"? Of course not! You would know that George's assertion that Johnny is a "chicken" means he believes Johnny is a coward. George, whether he knew it or not, used a metaphor, and you would understand the meaning of that metaphor. If you took George's statement literally or understood it to mean something else, you would be misinterpreting what he said.

Likewise, when Ecclesiastes says that men are "beasts" it is using a metaphor. The idea is that men are *like* beasts in important respects, and people need to learn that fact. To assume that the statement that people are "beasts" should be taken literally is to misinterpret the passage by taking something as literal which was meant to be figurative.

Consider the purpose of wisdom literature. Wisdom literature was intended to help human beings understand life and how to live it. In fact, "wisdom" in the Old Testament should be understood to mean, not just knowledge, but correct discernment leading to good decisions, resulting in the wise person's living right, or doing right, or thinking right, so that that person ends up being successful. Other books of the Bible were written to reveal God's eternal plan to save mankind from sin; the wisdom literature was written to help God's people live happy, successful lives here on earth. Consequently, this kind of literature contains sayings which are not law but which offer good advice, express emotions accurately, or state interesting facts.

We do the same thing today. We may say, for example, "Early to bed, early to rise, makes a man healthy, wealthy, and wise." Do we mean it? Will getting out of bed early guarantee that one will become rich? Of course not. But we use the saying because it offers good advice: It is a good idea to go to bed early and to get up early.

Sometimes the wisdom books may describe life as it is by using apparently contradictory statements.[7] Why? Because that is the way life is! That is the way we understand life to be! One who is wise needs to understand that fact.

For instance, sometimes we say, "Strike while the iron is hot!" And other times we say, "Haste makes waste!" Which is correct? Should you be in a hurry to get things done, or should you take things slower, being careful not to make any mistakes? The answer is: Both! Or: sometimes one, sometimes the other. Both offer good advice, but for different situations.

Likewise, when we find in Ecclesiastes or in the other books of wisdom strange or apparently contradictory statements, we need to interpret them

- in the light of other biblical teachings,
- recognizing that they may simply express how the author feels about an experience, or they may offer good advice for a particular situation.

Primarily we need to recognize that those sayings *are not intended to state an unbreakable law.*

Thus, when we read that we are not to be "excessively righteous," we conclude that the author is telling us something like: "Do not be so concerned about religious matters that you forget and neglect important things connected with everyday living. And do not make a big show of your religiosity."

"But," one might object, "if the statements in the books of wisdom are not law, if they simply offer only good advice or reflect the author's feelings or express shrewd observations about life, where does inspiration come in? I thought the law of God was inspired."

My answer: These books offer *inspired advice* (not necessarily law) and observations. "Haste makes waste" may offer good advice, but it is not *inspired* advice like the advice found in the Old Testament books of wisdom.

And the good thing about looking at Ecclesiastes and the other books of wisdom in this way is that—though you will not find in them many direct commands from God or much about how to be saved—you will find timely and timeless advice—advice which was good for the first readers of these books but which is equally helpful for us today. If we are wise, we will listen to the advice Ecclesiastes offers, take it to heart, and put it into practice, with the result that we will live happier, more fulfilling, more successful lives!

Conclusion

We began by saying that Ecclesiastes was intended to make you uncomfortable. How does it do that? What is it that makes your life meaningful? Your job? Your money—your prosperity? Power or fame? If so, Ecclesiastes is intended to shake you up, because it says that none of the above gives life meaning! Let me ask you: Are you satisfied with your life as it is? Getting up, going to work, making money, chasing fame and fortune, acquiring possessions, building things— without giving much thought to the fact that death and judgment await? Then maybe you ought not want to read the book of Ecclesiastes. It was designed to disturb you. To stop you in your tracks. To make you think about where you are going and how to get there. To challenge you to think about what really matters, what really gives meaning to life. Ecclesiastes was not intended to comfort. Someone said, "The preacher's job is to comfort the afflicted and afflict the comfortable." Are you ready to be afflicted? Read on.

Discussion Questions

1. In the title of this series, Ecclesiastes is described as a "document designed to disturb." To disturb whom? And why? Do you think it is possible that many people drift

through life, living from day to day without giving much thought to whether what they are doing is very meaningful? If so, do you think they need (we need?) to be "disturbed"?

2. Some things you should know about the book of Ecclesiastes: (1) Who wrote it? (2) What does the name mean? (3) How is it classified in the English Bible? In the Hebrew Bible? To what smaller classification does it belong? (4) Why is it classified among the books of "wisdom."? What other books are in this category? (5) What is the primary theme or purpose of the book?

3. You would do well, at the beginning of the study of any book of the Bible, to read through the entire book—preferably at one sitting—and try to decide what you think the book as whole is saying. If possible, do this with the book of Ecclesiastes, and come to class prepared to discuss your impression(s) of the book.

4. Discuss: Do you agree that a book of the Bible, or a passage in the Bible, may be inspired by God but not contain a law or laws which we must obey? What do you think about the idea that Ecclesiastes contains something like "inspired advice" rather than laws?

5. People have long said that one good thing
   about the books of wisdom is the timeless
   quality of the advice which they present. Do
   you agree? Can you think of examples of
   advice/suggestions/statements in those
   books which were true then and are still true
   today?

6. Ecclesiastes is about the meaning of life.
   What is life all about? What should be the
   most important thing in my life? Think
   about, and then discuss: What do you think is
   the most important thing in the lives of the
   people you know? What is the most
   important thing in your life? Look at the last
   few verses of Ecclesiastes to see Solomon's
   conclusion. Do you agree with him?

Endnotes

1. In part adapted from Coy Roper, *Notes on the Old
Testament* (Florence, AL: International Bible College,
1989, 1990, 1993, 1995), 100-101.

2. In this introduction we do not deal with the
inspiration of the text, or with its integrity or canonic-
ity. We believe that the book of Ecclesiastes was
inspired by God, that its text was transmitted without
major errors, and that it belongs in the canon of the
Old Testament. If one is concerned about such ques-

tions, he can find them discussed in conservative introductions to the Old Testament, such as Gleason Archer's *A Survey of Old Testament Introduction*.

3. The Septuagint is the Greek translation of the Hebrew Bible dating to the third century before Christ.

4. This idea, sometimes using other words (like "futile" or "futility") is found in about twenty-five verses in Ecclesiastes. See: 1:2, 14, 17; 2:1, 11, 15, 17, 21, 22, 23, 26; 3:19; 4:4, 6, 7, 8, 16; 5:10; 6:2, 9; 7:6; 8:14; 9:11; 11:8; 12:8.

5. See: 1:3, 14; 2:11, 17; 4:1, 7, 15; 5:13, 18; 8:15, 17; 9:3, 6, 9.

6. And since, in the mind of the writer, suicide is not an option—as it might be today for one who reaches the conclusion that life is meaningless.

7. A good example of this tendency is found in Proverbs 26:4, 5: "Do not answer a fool according to his folly, lest you be like him yourself. Answer a fool according to his folly, lest he be wise in his own eyes" (RSV). Does the book contradict itself? Which should you do? "Answer a fool according to his folly?" Or not? The answer would be: It depends. Sometimes it is better to do so, sometimes it is not.

2. What About Work?

We are talking about the meaning of life. What gives your life meaning? What is the most significant, most important thing in your life? From what do you get your greatest feeling of satisfaction? What makes you feel as if you matter, as if you are worth something to society?

The answer for many people, whether they want to admit it or not, would be: "My work."

Do you doubt it? Ask someone what he is and it is likely that he will reply, "A plumber … or a farmer … or an auto worker … or a fire fighter … or a teacher … or a custodian … or a lawyer." We think of ourselves in terms of our job, of our occupation. Our work defines us. And when we retire and no longer are occupied with work, we often feel lost and empty. Our life seems to have no purpose. Why? Because our work gives our life meaning.

"What's wrong with that?" you say.

The book of Ecclesiastes answers that question. What we call "work" it calls "toil" or "labor." But it makes plain that in Solomon's day, as in ours, many people lived to work, or to toil or labor, but their toil—after all was said and done—was meaningless; it was "vanity," a "striving after wind."

At the very beginning of the book the wise man says, "What advantage does a man have in all his work which he does under the sun?" (1:3). (Unless otherwise indicated, the version of the Bible quoted in this series is the New American Standard Bible (NASB)). The implied answer is "None!" It does no good to work or toil on this earth! Toil or labor is vain, or meaningless. It certainly does not make one's vain life meaningful.

Why?

Why Is Work Meaningless?

Why is work meaningless? According to Ecclesiastes, for at least six reasons.

First: Work is meaningless because it is painful. Ecclesiastes says that man gains nothing from his work except a life of pain and vexation:

For what does a man get in all his labor and in his striving with which he labors under the sun? Because all his days his task is painful and grievous; even at night his mind does not rest. This too is vanity (2:22,23).

If you do not believe that work can be painful and tiresome and grievous and that it can lead to worry at night, perhaps you have not worked enough or worked at enough different jobs.

Second: Work is meaningless because no matter how much money you make, you will never be satisfied. The book affirms that a man should work for a living, but Solomon says, "All a man's labor is for his mouth and yet the appetite is not satisfied" (6:7).

Man's "appetite is not satisfied." Do you believe it? How many people do you know who are completely happy with the money they make? How many would turn down a raise if they were offered one? No matter how much money we make, if we are asked, "How much would you like to make?", we are likely to answer, "Just a little more."

Third: Work is meaningless because the rewards of toil are vain. The point here is that we all want more, but even when we get it, and when we spend the additional money we have received, we find the results disappointing. The wise man writes:

All that my eyes desired I did not refuse them. I did not withhold my heart from any pleasure, for my heart was pleased because of all my labor and this was my reward for all my labor. Thus I considered all my activities which my hands had done and the labor which I had exerted, and behold all was vanity and striving after wind and there was no profit under the sun (2:10, 11).

Think about it: Five or ten years ago you wanted something, and maybe you said, "If only I could get this, I would be happy the rest of my life." Then you got it. Now, five or ten years later, are you perfectly happy? Or is there something else you want, something you just have to have? Or think about the people who, we might say, have "everything." Does all they own guarantee that they will be happy? You know it does not.

Fourth: Work is meaningless because everyone must die, and one cannot be sure what will happen regarding his accomplishments—especially the money he has made and saved—after his life is over.

For example, sometimes a man works hard all his life, but when he dies he has no one to leave his goods to. Therefore, he strives in vain. Solomon put it like this:

There was a certain man without a dependent, having neither a son nor a brother, yet there was no end to all his labor. Indeed his eyes were not satisfied with riches and he never asked, "And for whom am I laboring and depriving myself of pleasure?" This too is vanity and it is a grievous task (4:8).

Or even if he has someone to leave his wealth to, when one dies he may leave what he has toiled to get to someone who does not deserve it, who has not toiled for it. This is vanity, Solomon says.

When there is a man who has labored with wisdom, knowledge and skill, then he gives his legacy to one who has not labored with them. This too is vanity and a great evil (2:21).

Furthermore, work is in vain because when a man dies, the one he leaves his money to may be a fool.

Thus I hated all the fruit of my labor for which I had labored under the sun, for I must leave it to the man who will come after me. And who knows whether he will be a wise man or a fool? Yet he will have control over all the fruit of my labor for which I have labored by acting wisely under the sun. This too is vanity (2:18, 19).

Think about it: Is it not rather discouraging to know that when you die you will leave the money you

made by working to someone, and there is no guarantee as to what he or she will do with that money? You
may have saved your money; your heir might be a
spendthrift. You might have wanted your children to
live in the house you bought and fixed up or to main-
tain the family farm, but they may sell your place and
move away. You may be against drinking and gambling,
but your heirs might waste all your hard-earned money
on alcohol and playing poker. It is enough to make you
think "What's the good of working anyway?", is it not?

*Fifth: Work is meaningless because nothing ever really
changes—no matter how hard we work, life continues as
usual.* Solomon makes that point in one of the most
memorable passages in the book; he writes:

> What advantage does a man have in all his work
> which he does under the sun? A generation goes and
> a generation comes, but the earth remains forever.
> Also the sun rises and the sun sets; and hastening to
> its place it rises there again. Blowing toward the
> south, then turning to the north, the wind continues
> swirling along; and on its circular course the wind
> returns. All the rivers flow into the sea, yet the sea is
> not full. To the place where the rivers flow, there they
> flow again. All things are wearisome; man is not able
> to tell it. The eye is not satisfied with seeing, nor is
> the ear filled with hearing. That which has been is
> that which will be, and that which has been done is

that which will be done. So there is nothing new under the sun. Is there anything of which one might say, "See, this is new"? Already it has existed for ages which were before us (1:3–10).

Then in 3:1–9, Solomon elaborates on the theme that there is variety in life by saying that there is a time for everything under the sun, but that does not make life or work meaningful. He concludes, "What profit is there to the worker from that in which he toils?" The understood answer is "Nothing."

As further evidence that our work does not change anything, the author writes, "What is crooked cannot be straightened and what is lacking cannot be counted" (1:15).

Furthermore, Ecclesiastes implies that our decisions and our efforts make little difference because God has foreordained what will be, and nothing varies from His plans. Solomon says,

I know that everything that God does will remain forever; there is nothing to add to it and there is nothing to take from it, for God has so worked that man should fear Him. That which is has been already and that which will be has already been, for God seeks what has passed by (3:14,15).

Again, he writes:

Consider the work of God, for who is able to straighten what He has bent? In the day of prosperity be happy, but in the day of adversity consider—God has made the one as well as the other so that man will not discover anything that will be after him (7:13, 14).

Ecclesiastes says our efforts make little difference because God decides what will happen and we are not able to change His mind. Life goes on—the same things happen over and over again, just as God has decreed, and man cannot change anything. The book says, "Whatever has come to be has already been named, and a man is not able to dispute with one stronger than he" (6:10). To argue against one's fate is useless and simply increases the vanity (6:11).

We might want to argue with Solomon on this point. We might say, "I work—I live—to make a difference. And I think I do." Maybe so. But do you not also have dark moments when you are not so sure? I have been a preacher and teacher most of my life and sometimes I think that when I talk to a class or an audience I am talking into a vacuum. I am not sure anyone is listening. I cannot tell whether my words are being heard, whether they are changing anything, whether anything will be different because I preached and taught. Those are my dark moments.

I wonder if New Testament evangelists sometimes felt the same way. If you had been the preacher who began the work in Laodicea, for instance, how would you feel after it became known for its lukewarmness?

If you are in some other kind of occupation, is it not possible to feel that you have not really changed anything? Yes, you may have built someone a house, but did that make society any better? Is there any assurance that the people who live there will keep the house looking good? Does a new house guarantee that the people who live in it will be happy? Is the world really any different because of your construction business?

Again I say: In our darker moments, we often doubt that what we have done really makes much difference. We might agree with the wise man that our work, considered broadly at the end of our life, has been useless.

Sixth, work is meaningless because what we do under the sun is not long remembered. We read in 1:11, "There is no remembrance of earlier things; and also of the later things which will occur, there will be of them no remembrance."

Did you ever stop to think about how short people's memories are? Someone is a hero today, but tomorrow —or ten years from now—no one remembers him. We may do great work, but it is likely that our efforts will in the future be overlooked or forgotten. For instance, I have been in the business of preaching, as well as teaching in college, for many years. I remember preachers who were "famous" throughout the brotherhood (or large segments of the brotherhood) at one time, but now hardly anyone would remember them. I remember having teachers in college who were regarded as outstanding scholars and teachers, but now (almost) no one remembers them or their accomplishments. If you work in the hope that you will be remembered after you are dead and gone, you will probably be disappointed.

What About Our Work?

From all this, what should we conclude about our work?

We should *not* conclude that, since work is meaningless, we should not or need not work. Human beings were created to work and care for the rest of God's creation (Gen 2:15). The book of Proverbs extols the virtue of work (see, for instance, 10:4, 5, 26; 12:11, 24, 27; 13:4). In the New Testament, Jesus was a carpenter and His disciples were chosen from the working class. The apostle Paul worked as a tentmaker. Christians were commanded: "He who steals must steal no longer; but rather he must labor, performing with his own hands what is good, so that he will have something to share with one who has need" (Eph 4:28). Apparently, some in Thessalonica had the idea that since Christ's second coming would be very soon, they could quit work. Paul dealt with their misunderstanding and told them they were to work for a living. In fact, he said, "If anyone is not willing to work, then he is not to eat, either" (2 Thess 3:10b).

From the negative comments about work in the book of Ecclesiastes, should we conclude that we should be lazy? That we should live off others or off the government when we are able to make a living for ourselves? No! But we should learn this: If work is all that gives your life meaning, you are bound to end up disappointed and disillusioned. If your work, your toil, is all that is important to you, at the end of your life you will probably say, or think, "All is vanity and a striving after wind."

Yes, work is necessary; work is good, but that is not all there is to living. If you think it is, you have problems; your life, says Solomon, is meaningless. That is part of the disturbing news from the book of Ecclesiastes.

Discussion Questions

1. How important is your work, your job, your occupation, to you? Do you define yourself by what you do for a living? How important do you think work is to others? Do you know people who seem to live to work rather than to work to live?

2. What does the Old Testament teach about one's responsibility to work to support

himself? What does the New Testament teach on the subject? Considering these teachings, do you think a Christian would ever be justified to live off others (to live on welfare, for example) if he or she was physically and mentally capable of working? Discuss what you think should be done about the problem of people who could work work but don't—who beg for food, for instance.

3. The Bible requires us to work (see above), but Ecclesiastes says that our toil is vain or meaningless. How can we reconcile those two facts? Do you think it is possible to work for a living—even to be a good, hard worker who succeeds at the job he or she does—and still lead a meaningful life? How would a Christian do it? Would it have something to do with priorities? Maybe the Christian's work would be very important, but not have priority over spiritual things? What do you think? If so, what would that mean in real life? Can you think of an example of how a successful worker might have to choose between his/her job and his/her religious obligations?

4. Are there some kinds of work the Christian ought not engage in? If so, what?

3. What About Wisdom?

What about wisdom? Does being wise give meaning to an otherwise meaningless existence "under the sun"?

A student of Ecclesiastes might be inclined to answer that question in the affirmative. After all, Ecclesiastes is one of the "books of wisdom" (the others are Job, Proverbs, and Song of Solomon)—books which promote wisdom, which make clear the value of being wise. And Ecclesiastes itself declares that wisdom is good. The wise man said;

- "Wisdom excels folly as light excels darkness" (2:13).
- God gives "wisdom, knowledge and joy" to those who are "good in His sight" (2:26).
- "A poor yet wise lad is better than an old king

who no longer knows how to receive instruction" (4:13).

- "It is better to listen to the rebuke of a wise man than for one to listen to the song of fools" (7:5).
- "Wisdom along with an inheritance is good … wisdom is protection just as money is protection, but the advantage of knowledge is that wisdom preserves the lives of its possessors" (7:11, 12).
- "A man's wisdom illumines him and causes his stern face to beam" (8:1b).
- "Words from the mouth of a wise man are gracious" (10:12a).

Obviously Solomon believed in and taught the value of wisdom.

Nevertheless, he also taught that wisdom is vain or meaningless. Look at Ecclesiastes 1:16–18:

And I said to myself, "Behold, I have magnified and increased wisdom more than all who were over Jerusalem before me; and my mind has observed a wealth of wisdom and knowledge." And I set my mind to know wisdom and to know madness and folly; I realized that this also is striving after wind. Because in much wisdom there is much grief and increasing knowledge results in increasing pain.

Does that sound strange? Solomon, known as the wisest mortal who ever lived, concluded that increasing wisdom and enjoying a wealth of knowledge is "striving after wind." Why?

That is a question we need to consider. We live in an age in which education is highly valued. Children are taught to finish high school. High school graduates are urged to go on to college. People who go to college are frequently not satisfied with one degree. Many continue on to get one or more graduate degrees. Does it not sound strange, even disturbing, when Ecclesiastes says that this thirst for knowledge and wisdom is nothing more than "striving after wind"—that it is vain, meaningless?

So we ask again: Why? Why is wisdom meaningless? Ecclesiastes provides at least five answers to that question.

One: Being wise is vain because wisdom increases vexation. Ecclesiastes 1:18 says, "In much wisdom there is much grief and increasing knowledge results in increasing pain." In other words, the wiser you get, the more you know, the more pain and grief you experience.

How could that be? Solomon does not explain, but we can come up with an answer. "Ignorance is bliss," we sometimes say, and it often is. The more you know about what it takes to stay healthy, the more different things you worry about: Am I eating too much? Am I eating the right things? Am I getting enough exercise? Should I go to the doctor about this symptom? You might, as a result of asking those questions, save yourself from pain of sickness, but you have added worries to your life that the happy-go-lucky ignorant individual does not experience. (He may die sooner, but he may live with fewer worries.) In the same way, there are all kinds of potential dangers about us that only the knowledgeable—maybe the scientists—are aware of. Their great knowledge may cause them pain; our ignorance leaves us blissfully unaware. It is often true: The more you know, the more you have to worry about.

Another way that wisdom or knowledge can bring vexation today is the more you know—sometimes the more education you have—the more is expected of you.

(I doubt that Solomon had this in mind, but my close friends and kinfolks can testify that their knowledge causes them vexation when I, being altogether technologically inept, bring my computer to them with a problem that I cannot fix—and they fix it in three minutes. I expect that when they see me coming they think, "I wish I did not know anything about computers! How much time and trouble it would save me!")

Two: Being wise is vain because one cannot find out all there is to know. No doubt it is good to be inquisitive—to be curious—to want to know more—to be someone who continues to learn, no matter how old one gets. The writer of Ecclesiastes was like that. He searched for

the truth. He wanted to know. And if we believe that
Solomon was the writer, then we have to believe that he
did in fact learn much. However, Solomon tells us that
one frustrating aspect of wisdom is that, as much as
you may learn, there are some things that you will
never figure out. Notice these scriptures:

- He has made everything appropriate in its
  time. He has also set eternity in their heart,
  yet so that man will not find out the work
  which God has done from the beginning even
  to the end (3:11).
- For who knows what is good for a man
  during his lifetime, during the few years of
  his futile life? He will spend them like a
  shadow. For who can tell a man what will be
  after him under the sun? (6:12)
- No one knows what will happen … (8:7a).
- I tested all this with wisdom, and I said, "I
  will be wise," but it was far from me. What
  has been is remote and exceedingly
  mysterious. Who can discover it? (7:23, 24)
- When I gave my heart to know wisdom and
  to see the task which has been done on the
  earth (even though one should never sleep
  day or night), and I saw every work of God, I
  concluded that man cannot discover the work

which has been done under the sun. Even
though man should seek laboriously, he will
not discover; and though the wise man should
say, "I know," he cannot discover (8:16, 17).

Our first reaction to those passages, if we have been
to school or college and studied for final exams or
comprehensives or tried to solve a research problem,
might be "Amen!" It is hard to find out, and hard to
remember, answers to our questions. But the writer of
Ecclesiastes is saying more than this. It was hard to
learn enough to pass that final, but we did learn it and
we passed it. Solomon, in contrast, is saying that as
much as we may learn through study and contempla-
tion, there are some things we will never learn.

We will never fully understand the work of God—
what He has done and is doing—; we cannot be altogether certain what is the best course for an individual;
and even if we were to study day and night we could
not discover all the mysteries of this universe that God
has made.

I expect many of us have felt this kind of frustration.
We study, we work, we try to learn more and more, but
we still do not know as much as we think we need to
know. In fact, as the saying goes, "the more we know,
the more we know we don't know." The inability to
understand the facts of nature, the makeup of the

universe, the reasons why people act as they do, etc., may be extremely frustrating.

When we add to that the fact that we never know—no matter how hard we try to predict the future—what is going to happen to us, makes life—even if one has acquired wisdom and knowledge—even more troubling. Maybe you know quantum physics, but do you know what will happen tomorrow? Maybe you are the wisest man on earth, but are you wise enough to predict when the next pandemic will break out, or whether you will live to see the New Year?

Wisdom has its limitations. And one of those is that it does not guarantee that we will know everything, or even everything we want to know. That, says Ecclesiastes, makes the acquisition of wisdom vain or meaningless.

Three: Being wise is vain because wisdom does not really change anything. The book of Ecclesiastes says that, no matter what we do, or how wise we are, nothing changes much. Solomon wrote, "So I turned to consider wisdom, madness and folly; for what will a man do who comes after the king except what has already been done?" (2:12)

One might be inclined to argue with Solomon on this point. Have not new inventions—created, we might say, by the application of wisdom—changed our lives for the better?

In defense of Solomon's argument we might reply:

Yes, we now have automobiles and computers and smart phones, but is it not also true that summer comes and winter goes, that the sun rises and sets, that natural disasters still occur, that human beings live longer but are not necessarily happier, that sorrow and suffering still exist and wars are still fought? In other words, for all man's wisdom and new inventions, life remains much the same. Thus, trying to increase your wisdom and knowledge could be seen as a waste of time, as vain or meaningless.

Four: Being wise is vain because wisdom does not protect us from the problems of life and death. Solomon asks, "For what advantage does the wise man have over the fool?" (6:8a) The understood answer is: None! The wise man has no advantage over the fool! In what sense? We might be able to think of a number of advantages to being wise rather than foolish, so in what sense does the wise man have no advantage over the fool?

In the sense that the wise man, like the fool, must experience the problems that come with living on this earth. Suppose that you have a Ph.D. Will that keep your car from breaking down? Will it keep you from getting sick? Will it guarantee that your house will not be blown away by a tornado? Does it provide assurance that you will not die young? In fact, the major reason why the writer of Ecclesiastes says that wisdom is vain is that the wise man must someday die, just as the fool does. He writes,

And yet I know that one fate befalls them both [both the wise man and the foolish man]. Then I said to myself, "As is the fate of the fool, it will also befall me. Why then have I been extremely wise?" So I said to myself, "This too is vanity." ... the wise man and the fool alike die! (2:14b, 15, 16b).

There is some value in being wise, but you cannot depend on your wisdom or knowledge guarding you from all the ills that the flesh is heir to—and your wisdom will not keep your from dying! Thus, you could say that wisdom is useless, meaningless, vain.

Five: Being wise is vain because the wise man is not likely to be remembered after his death. Ecclesiastes says, "For there is no lasting remembrance of the wise man as with the fool, inasmuch as in the coming days all will be forgotten" (2:16a). As usual, the writer employs hyperbole—exaggeration or overstatement—to make his point. The fact is most people are remembered, at least by someone, at least for a while. But memories tend to fade. We eventually forget. Even those who were famous in their own time are likely to be remembered by fewer and fewer people. For example, when I was a kid I was a New York Yankees fan. How many people remember the Yankee players from the 1950s? Joe Demaggio? Maybe. Mickey Mantle. Perhaps. Yori Berra? Possibly. Phil Rizzuto? Unlikely. The sports stars who make headlines today are mostly forgotten tomorrow.

Or think about the pyramids of Egypt. They were built as monuments to Egyptian kings, to Pharaohs. We all remember that there are pyramids. Do we remember the names of the Pharaohs they were built to honor?

What is true of baseball stars and Pharaohs is also true of those who are wise. I expect that many inventors have made headlines in their own day, only to be forgotten by history. On a personal level: Think of one who seeks to be wise, or to gain knowledge—say, by continuing his education. How long after his death will he be remembered for his wisdom or knowledge?

In other words, if you want to be wise in order to be remembered from now on, forget it. The wise man, like the fool, is soon forgotten. So says Solomon.

Conclusion

What shall we say to all this? How does it apply today?

We should not conclude that God places a premium on ignorance, or that it is a sin to get an advanced degree, or that a Christian does not need a secular education. God chose the well-educated Saul of Tarsus to be an apostle. And He expects us, as stewards of all He has bestowed on us, to use all our gifts to best advantage—including our mental ability—to serve mankind and to glorify Him. In practical terms, that means we should use our brainpower in the best way possible. We should be as wise as possible so that we can help advance God's kingdom and make life on earth better for other human beings. (For ten-year-old boys, it means, "Do your homework!")

But, while the vanity of wisdom should not keep us from seeking wisdom and knowledge, it should keep us from depending on earthly wisdom and knowledge to give everlasting meaning to life. If "wisdom" is our answer to the question, "What gives life under the sun meaning?", we fail the test.

The New Testament makes that point emphatically when it condemns dependence on worldly wisdom. For instance, the apostle Paul wrote, "Has not God made foolish the wisdom of the world?" (1 Cor 1:20b; see the context from 1:18 through 2:16, where human wisdom is contrasted with godly wisdom). If we hope to save ourselves by becoming wise according to the standards of this world, we will be eternally disappointed.

Nevertheless, according to the New Testament, there are some things we should know if we hope to be saved. For one, we should know the truth, for that will make us free (John 8:32). For another, we should know God—that is, we should have not only an understanding of God but also a good relationship with Him. If we do not know God, we are warned that "the Lord Jesus will be revealed from heaven with His mighty angels in flaming fire, dealing out retribution to all *who do not know God* and to those who do not obey the gospel our Lord Jesus. These will pay the penalty of eternal destruction from the presence of the Lord and from the glory of His power" (2 Thess 1:7–9).

What about the wisdom of this world—the endless pursuit of knowledge, the determination to be wise "under the sun"? It is "vanity" and "a striving after wind."

What about getting to know God and His Son Jesus Christ? It results in freedom from sin and guilt in this world and eternal joy in another!

If you were forced to make a choice, which would you choose?

Discussion Questions

1. Wisdom and knowledge are closely connected in Ecclesiastes and the other Old Testament wisdom books. In our society, do you think that a person could have "knowledge"—for example, an advanced education—but not have "wisdom"? On the other hand, do you think there are people in our society who have "wisdom" even though

they have little "knowledge" (formal education)? Today, which is better? Which would you rather have? "Wisdom" or "knowledge" (formal education)?

2. Is it possible that the attainment of wisdom, or knowledge, today might be regarded as useless? For instance, might one be smart, or knowledgeable, or wise, but not listened to by others? Is it possible that one might get a formal education—a college degree—but still not succeed in life? If so, might this make one feel that the acquisition of wisdom is meaningless?

3. Does wisdom—however you define it— guarantee success in life?

4. Will wisdom keep one from doing wrong, from sinning? To answer that, think of the example of Solomon himself. Is it possible that the acquisition of knowledge through education, or knowing that one is "wise" might lead to a person's being puffed up or conceited, that it might cause him to "think too highly of himself"? What might be the detrimental effects of such a feeling? What do you think might keep this from happening to someone who is aware that he is, say, smarter than most other people?

4. What About Pleasure?

What about pleasure? Does pleasure make life meaningful? In his search to find meaning in an otherwise vain life, Solomon turned to pleasure. He wrote:

I said to myself, "Come now, I will test you with pleasure. So enjoy yourself." And behold, it too was futility. I said of laughter, "It is madness," and of pleasure, "What does it accomplish?" I explored with my mind how to stimulate my body with wine while my mind was guiding me wisely, and how to take hold of folly, until I could see what good there is for the sons of men to do under heaven the few years of their lives. (2:1–3)[1]

Solomon's Experience With Pleasure

If anyone could test whether pleasure gives meaning to life, Solomon could. He was rich and powerful. To use modern terms, he could buy anything he wanted. He had everything anyone might want. He not only had riches and material goods; he also enjoyed fame and glory. He was a great king! And he had, the Bible says, a thousand wives and concubines—a thousand sexual partners!

A lot of people today assume that if they could enjoy the sexual favors of as many different individuals of the opposite sex as possible—if they could, for example, have sexual relations with a thousand others—that would be the pinnacle of pleasure; it would be paradise on earth! As far as they are concerned, that alone would make life enjoyable, successful, and meaningful!

But Solomon concluded that pleasure is vain or futile. Why? Ecclesiastes does not say. However, the Old Testament does reveal that Solomon, in spite of the fact that he had been so wonderfully blessed by God, fell away and worshiped other gods in his old age. The result was that God told him that He was going to take most of the tribes of Israel away from Solomon's son and give them to another. In other words, Solomon knew before he died that, because of his sin, his kingdom would be divided and someone who was not his descendant would reign over most of it. That knowledge would have not made him happy. It might even have caused him to think that his life was all in vain.

In addition, Solomon, because of his unfaithfulness to God in his later years, faced a number of adversaries whom God raised up against him. Again, it is possible that those adversaries made life so miserable for Solomon that he decided that, in spite of the pleasures he had enjoyed, life was all in vain. Life had no meaning.

Our Experience With Pleasure

We seek for pleasure. Human beings seek a pleasurable life—an enjoyable, happy life. (There may be exceptions to that rule—people who think that to please God they must live in a state of continual penance, never smiling or laughing but always bemoaning their sins. But people with such beliefs are probably very few.)

We seek for pleasure in a hundred ways. Children play games—they may play board games, or play "pretend," or chase one another through the house. Young people amuse themselves by "hanging out" together, maybe by driving cars too fast or doing other dangerous things, or sometimes by playing sports or going to movies. As adults we may play golf or go bowling, or go shopping, or spend time getting our hair done, or travel or go on vacations or visit exotic places, or go hunting or fishing. And when we get old we may find our greatest pleasure in visiting with family and watching television or playing games on a computer. And at almost every age we find pleasure in satisfying the fleshly desires we were born with—our desire for food and rest, for instance, and our sexual desires. In all these ways we seek and find pleasure.

There is nothing wrong with seeking and finding pleasure. From a biblical standpoint—as we shall assert in a later lesson—the Bible does not teach that it is wrong for human beings to be happy, to experience pleasure. In fact, one theme of the book of Ecclesiastes is that we should employ wisdom to enjoy our life on earth.

God made humanity with a capacity for enjoying life, and He placed us in a world where there is much to enjoy, much to give us happiness. He therefore intended for us, ideally, to enjoy ourselves, to be, as a rule, happy, to experience pleasure, rather than constant and unrelenting sadness and sorrow.

The Wrong Experience of Pleasure

Solomon's search for pleasure did not bring him lasting happiness or fulfillment; it did not make his life meaningful. Similarly, our striving for pleasure may lead, not to lasting happiness, but to disappointment or sorrow. It might even have catastrophic consequences. Seeking pleasure then becomes a bad experience with unhappy results which make life meaningless. How could that happen to us?

By seeking pleasure in the wrong way. One way that seeking pleasure could produce unhappiness is that we might seek pleasure in the wrong way. That was Solomon's major problem. Contrary to the revealed will of God, he married many foreign women, and when he was old those foreign women—who worshiped other gods—turned Solomon's heart away from the one true God—the Lord God of Israel—and he offered sacrifices to the foreign gods his wives worshiped (1 Kgs 11). Because of that sin, God took away most of the kingdom from Solomon's son. Solomon sought pleasure by having many foreign wives as sexual partners, but he found God's displeasure, which resulted in his descendants forfeiting most of the kingdom over which he reigned.

Similarly, seeking pleasure today may lead to sin, sorrow, and shame. The New Testament warns against seeking happiness in the wrong way.

For example, when Jesus explained the parable of the sower, He said that "the seed which fell among thorns, these are the ones who have heard, and as they go on their way they are choked with worries and riches and pleasures of this life and bring no fruit to maturity" (Luke 8:14). Seeking pleasure in the wrong way keeps the Christian from bearing fruit.

Again, Hebrews 11 describes Moses' choice to

believe in and obey God in these words: "Moses when he was grown up refused to be called the son of Pharaoh's daughter, choosing rather to endure ill-treatment with the people of God than to enjoy the passing pleasures of sin" (Heb 11:24, 25). Moses chose faith in God over "the passing pleasures of sin." Too many people choose the "passing pleasures of sin" over God.

Another example: When He told the story of the prodigal son, Jesus said that the prodigal asked for his share of the inheritance, and once he had it he took his leave of his home and went into a far country where he wasted what he had in "riotous living" (Luke 15, KJV). No doubt he was enjoying himself; he was living for pleasure. But his pleasure produced no good results: he ended up in a pig pen! The moral of the story? Seeking pleasure in the wrong way can push you into a life of sin! You could end up, metaphorically speaking, in a pig pen!

Just as in these examples, our search for pleasure can bring disappointment, disillusionment, disaster. Someone thinks that if he can accumulate more money, he can find happiness. But the usual means of making money are too slow for him, so he tries dishonest means, and his search for pleasure lands him in jail. Others deliberately choose a life of crime in order to find pleasure, and they end up behind bars or dead! Many people, young and old, get the idea that they can find pleasure in alcohol or illegal drugs or gambling, but they end up as addicts, ruining their lives, maybe even committing suicide. And many seek pleasure from illicit and immoral sexual activity. They may enjoy the "passing pleasures of sin" for a time, but they end up ruining lives. Their amorous activities may result in unplanned pregnancies, contracting sexually transmitted diseases, divorces, and broken homes and neglected children.

We should not be surprised that the search for pleasure results in sin. After all, that is how the devil lures us to do his will.

Maybe you have been to a carnival and have walked down the midway and have seen the barkers standing in front of their tents hustling their wares. "Come on in, folks. See the fattest man on earth, the smallest woman, a dog with two heads! For only a dollar! No better bargain anywhere! Come on in for an evening of enjoyment!"

That is what the devil does. He stands in front of those sinful experiences and cries out, "Come on in, folks! Drink as much as you want! Sex anytime, anyplace, with anyone! Steal and lie and loaf on the job and get rich doing it! And all the fun that goes with drugs and alcohol and gambling! This is the way to happiness! To fulfillment, to meaning! Come on in and enjoy yourself! No cost to you! It's all free!"

The devil lies, of course. There is a cost to be paid for indulging in those sins so that you can find pleasure. Ultimately, the cost is your soul! Immediately, it is unhappiness and futility and a meaningless life!

By seeking pleasure as one's main goal in life. The search for pleasure does not, in addition, give meaning to life when it becomes the main goal of one's life—for two reasons:

First, it is impossible to go through life without experiencing anything but pleasure. Sometimes we act as if we think the only thing we should expect in life is happiness and joy and peace and satisfaction. If hard times come, if sickness affects others, if some go broke, we assume that those things will not happen to us. We are focused on pleasure; nothing unpleasant could happen to us!

But if you think about it, you know that premise is untrue: You cannot live long without experiencing trouble of some sort. You or someone in your family will get sick. There will be a car accident. You will suffer because of the weather—tornadoes or hurricanes or earthquakes or floods or drought. You may lose your job and be unable to get another. A recession or depression may affect you. Your house burns down. You lose a crop of wheat because of a hailstorm. Your puppy dog dies. You know such things happen. You know you are not immune; they could happen to you. You have stood beside the coffin or the graveside of a loved one. Bad things happen.

(Looking back on my life, I remember when, about

the time I started to high school, our family moved from one small town in Oklahoma to another. During the year and a half we lived there my brother had a wreck in a '39 Ford we owned—he rolled the car three times—fortunately without being hurt seriously—; Dad also had a wreck, driving another car into a ditch when he went to sleep coming home from working the grave-yard shift; our well went dry; our garage—which was full of our furniture and other things we had stored—burned down; a fat lamb which had won first place at the state fair was attacked by an angry sow and had its ear torn off; my brother got sick and spent about six weeks in the hospital. If we had been living for plea-sure, we would not have found much fulfillment during that period of time. You may have had a series of misadventures like that yourself, when you certainly could not say that you were living for pleasure.)

The book of Job says, "Man that is born of a woman is of few days and full of trouble" (Job 14:1, KJV). If you have lived any time on this earth, you will say "Amen" to those sentiments! And, given that fact, the person who lives only for pleasure is bound to be frustrated because "into each life" some trouble must come. That is one reason why seeking pleasure as your main goal in life will not be a successful endeavor; it will not give life meaning.

A second reason why making pleasure our main goal in life is a mistake is that, at the end of life, we know that—even if we have not sought to find pleasure from sinning, and even if we have lived a relatively happy life, without many major problems—living for pleasure does not satisfy our inborn, deep-down sense of values.

Think about it like this: Imagine that you are living for pleasure. And you get the greatest pleasure out of playing golf. So you play golf three or four or five times a week. You get pretty good. You may even win a local tournament or two. At the end of your life, on your deathbed, are you going to be satisfied with your life if all you have accomplished is to be a pretty good golfer? Maybe your obituary would read, in part: "Here lies Joe Smith. He played golf five times a week, about ten thousand times during his lifetime. He was good at golf, usually getting pars and bogeys. He won two local tournaments. But he never helped his neighbors. He was a stranger to his wife and an absentee father while his children were growing up. The neighborhood deteriorated while he lived there. He did not attend church, did not give money to help the poor, did not visit the sick, did not try to encourage the depressed, paid no active role in the local school or community. But he was a good golfer and derived great pleasure from that fact."

Would you want that to be your obituary—though you might need to substitute something else for golfing —like hunting or fishing or shopping or watching TV? I doubt that you would want an obituary that read like that. Why? Because we all know instinctively that there is more to life than play, that being a good golfer or shopper or softball player does not give life meaning, that we were put here on earth for a different purpose —a higher purpose—than just finding pleasure by seeing how many fish we could catch or how many shopping malls we could visit.

In other words, the person who spends his or her life seeking pleasure as his or her primary goal, or only goal, at the end of life will probably ask: "What good did I do with my life? How did I make a difference? Yes, I bowled three perfect games in forty years, but in the long run, what difference does that make?"

Even under the best of circumstances, the person who has lived for pleasure will end up agreeing with Solomon: This, too, is vanity and striving after wind. There is value in being happy, but making pleasure the only important thing in your life is to live a vain and empty and purposeless life!

The Right Experience of Pleasure

Nevertheless—in spite of all the negative things we have said about pleasure—there is a time and place or pleasure, enjoyment, happiness, in our lives, as long as we do not make worldly pleasure the main reason for our existence. The last several lessons in this series describe what Ecclesiastes says about how we can enjoy life even in a meaningless universe.

But when we as Christians think about what will, or ought to, make us—and our friends—truly happy, what will bring the greatest pleasure, we need to think about something else—namely, about being saved from sin.

We all are sinners (Rom 3:23), and sin condemns us (Rom 6:23). We may think living a sinful life will bring happiness here in this life—and to some extent it might; there is such a thing as the "passing pleasure" of sin—but the fact is that sin separates us from God now (Isa 59:1, 2) and will cause us to be punished by Him eternally.

How can we escape such a fate? Not naturally. It does not happen as a matter of course to everyone. Not by living a good moral life. Morality or good works will never make up for our sins; it will never remove the guilty stain of sin from our souls. How then? We have to be, as the song says, "washed in the blood of the Lamb"—Jesus Christ, the Lamb of God, who takes away the sins of the world.

When or how does that happen? When we respond to the gospel as people did in the first century—when, after hearing the gospel preached, we respond with faith and repent of our sins and are baptized in water for the remission of sins (Acts 2:38).

At that time our sins are forgiven. And at that time,

perhaps more than at any other in this world, we experience real pleasure, true happiness, genuine rejoicing!

After the Ethiopian eunuch was baptized, he "went on his way rejoicing" (Acts 8:39). So can we. And that is the way to true happiness, to genuine lasting pleasure.

Discussion Questions

1. What do you think about the proposition that pleasure, or happiness, or enjoyment, is regarded as the greatest good by most people in the modern world? What evidence is there that this is the case? Do people today expect to suffer? Do we think something is dreadfully wrong if we hurt or have any kind of problems?

2. What about the "pleasures of sin"? Consider the teaching of 1 John 2:15–17. Can you think of biblical examples of people who fell because of the pleasures sin promises? Can you think of examples in today's world of how sin is pleasurable but in the end is destructive? How can one resist the temptation to say "yes" to the pleasures of sin?

3. Do you derive "pleasure"—or enjoyment, or happiness—from your religion? Should you? Is Christianity intended to bring nothing but

"doom and gloom" into its practitioners' lives? If you don't enjoy being and living as a Christian, what can you do about it so that you can "rejoice always"?

4. And do you enjoy Christian worship? Do you think most Christians do? Should we as Christ's disciples and God's children enjoy worshiping? Enjoy singing hymns, for example? If we don't, why don't we? What could be done to solve this problem?

Endnotes

1. Solomon also mentions seeking pleasure in 2:8 and 2:10.

5. What About Riches?

What about riches? Does making money—especially a lot of money—give meaning to life? I suspect that many believe that it does. I know that their actions indicate that they think that making money and having money—or having the things that money can buy—is the most important thing in the world.

How about you? Do you spend all your energy trying to make more and more money? Is that your chief concern? Do you especially respect and honor those who are rich? Are you inclined to look down on those who are poor? Is the possession of money and the things that money can buy your primary concern in life?

If we think that money gives life meaning, we will have to disagree with Solomon. In spite of the fact that he was remarkably rich, he pronounced the acquisition of wealth as meaningless. He wrote, "I collected for myself silver and gold and the treasure of kings ... . All that my eyes desired I did not refuse them ... and behold all was vanity and striving after wind and there was no profit under the sun" (2:8, 10, 11).

Why was seeking wealth like striving after the wind? Why did riches not give life meaning? Let us consider two or three passages from Ecclesiastes to answer that question.

What Ecclesiastes Says About Riches

Let us begin by reading from Ecclesiastes 2:

> I bought male and female slaves and I had homeborn slaves. And I possessed flocks and herds larger than all who preceded me in Jerusalem. Also, I collected for myself silver and gold and the treasure of kings and provinces. I provided for myself male and female singers and the pleasures of men—many concubines ... . All that my eyes desired I did not refuse them. I did not withhold my heart from any pleasure, for my heart was pleased because of all my labor and this was my reward for all my labor. Thus I considered all my activities which my hands had done ... and behold all was vanity and striving after wind and there was no profit under the sun (2:7, 8, 10, 11).

In this passage we are impressed with the fact that Solomon was rich. He had flocks and herds, silver and gold and other treasures, and as many concubines as he wanted. In fact, he was richer than any king who had preceded him. If you want to be rich, there are any number of people in the world today who could provide you with a model of wealth, but none would have been more wealthy than Solomon.

Yet Solomon says that his acquisition of wealth was vain. Why? He does not tell us in these verses, but he does suggest several reasons why riches do not, in and of themselves, give one's life meaning in other passages. Notice Ecclesiastes 5:10–17:

He who loves money will not be satisfied with money, nor he who loves abundance with its income. This, too, is vanity. When good things increase, those who consume them increase. So what is the advantage to their owners except to look on? The sleep of the working man is pleasant, whether he eats little or much; but the full stomach of the rich man does not allow him to sleep. There is a grievous evil which I have seen under the sun: riches being hoarded by their owner to his hurt. When those riches were lost through a bad investment and he had fathered a son, then there was nothing to support him. As he had come naked from his mother's womb, so will he return as he came. He will take nothing from the fruit of his labor that he can carry in his hand. This also is a grievous evil—exactly as a man is born, thus will he die. So what is the advantage to him who toils for the wind? Throughout his life he also eats in darkness with great vexation, sickness and anger (5:10–17).

Consider also 6:1, 2:

There is an evil which I have seen under the sun and it is prevalent among men—a man to whom God has given riches and wealth and honor so that his soul lacks nothing of all that he desires; yet God has not empowered him to eat from them, for a foreigner enjoys them. This is vanity and a severe affliction (6:1, 2).

These passages teach that the person who puts making money first on his or her "to do" list, thinking that it will make life meaningful, is mistaken for at least seven reasons:

First, if riches are your goal, you will never get enough to satisfy you. "He who loves money will not be satisfied with money" (5:10). If acquiring wealth is your goal, how much will it take to make you happy? I suspect that if that describes you, you would be like the big farmer who was asked, "You've got 10,000 acres; how much more land do you want?" He replied, "Not much. Just the land adjoining mine."

Whoever the person is whose goal it is to get rich—ask him or her how much he or she needs, and you are likely to hear, "Not much. Just a little more." The need for "a little more" will always be there. No matter how large our crop, we will always want to build "bigger barns" (Luke 12) to store even more crops.

And knowing that you never have enough to satisfy will—if you are depending on riches—make life dissatisfying—and meaningless—in other words, vain.

Second, if you succeed at getting rich you will discover that many others are rich also. "When good things increase those who consume them increase" (5:11). Perhaps the writer is saying that, even if you acquire riches you will discover that you are not alone. Many others are rich, and some will be richer than you. That may be disillusioning.

Or maybe he is saying that if you acquire riches there will always be some who will "consume" them—maybe tax collectors, or those you pay rent to, or the merchants you buy from. (Or, maybe, if you win the lottery, or the Publishers Clearing House prize, lots of friends and relatives you did not know you had.) All prosper because you are rich—and all you can do is sit back and watch them "consume" your wealth. Being rich is, I suppose, an expensive thing. That would also tend to make being rich rather meaningless.

Third, riches are not always good for a man. "The full stomach of the rich man does not allow him to sleep"

(5:12). Riches can be "hoarded" by the owner "to his hurt" (5:13). If one acquires riches as his main aim in life, he may be tempted to use those riches in ways that are detrimental to his (or his family's) wellbeing. He might, as Solomon suggests, eat too much with the result that he cannot sleep at night—or eating too much could have other negative effects. He might indulge in worldly pleasures—drinking, gambling, drugs, or, like Solomon, concubines or prostitutes—that he could not afford if he did not have a lot of money. (Haven't we all heard of famous rich people who died at a relatively young age because of drug addiction or drug overdoses?) There are some problems that the poor are likely to have, but others that only those who are rich are likely to suffer from.

Thus, if one lives to make money, then uses that money in hurtful ways, his success in getting rich is "vanity and striving after wind."

Fourth, riches can be lost. "Those riches were lost through a bad investment" (5:14). This fact has to be one of the scariest facts that accompany getting rich: "I found these riches; I can lose them. My wealth came to me quickly and easily; it can leave just as quickly and easily." Nothing that is physical and material in this world has any guarantee of continuance. One week you are riding high with a new high-paying job; the next week you lose that job. Or you have money invested in the stock market—enough to make you rich—and then the market crashes, and suddenly you have one-tenth of what you had before. You build a beautiful vacation home in the wilderness—and it is destroyed by a forest fire. You have a lovely expensive house on the beach— and a hurricane or tidal wave destroys it.

The moral of the story? Making the possession of earthly things your goal in life is meaningless because you can lose it all in a second.

The Bible attests to that fact. James said that your plans for tomorrow could easily be overturned because "you do not know what your life will be like tomorrow" (Jas 4:13, 14). How about the rich man who built bigger barns so that he could take it easy in the future? God said to him, "You fool! This very night your soul is required of you" (Luke 12:20). At the height of his reign over Babylon, Belshazzar received this message from the Lord God, through Daniel His prophet: "You have been weighed on the scales and found deficient … .Your kingdom has been divided and given to the Medes and Persians" (Dan 5:27, 28).

Both Bible testimony and personal experience tell us that it is foolish to depend on wealth to give life meaning, because riches can be lost.

Fifth, when one dies, his or her riches must be left behind. "As he came naked from his mother's womb, so will he return" (5:15, 16). Or as we might say: "You can't take it with you when you die."

To Solomon, perhaps the most meaningful thing

about life is death. One who has been born will eventually die. We all die. We all go to the same place, at least in the sense that we all go into graves. And after we are dead, what difference does it make? What difference does it make whether you were tall or short? Good-looking or ugly? Rich or poor? A worker or a boss? Male or female? We all die. Therefore, what we do on this earth, in this life, "under the sun," makes little difference. The poor man may have a small funeral or none at all; the rich man may have a large expensive funeral. But the rich man is just as dead as the poor man. So what difference does it make whether you are rich or not? Trying to get rich makes no sense because even if you succeed, you end up in the grave.

"But," someone might object, "if you are rich when you die, you have the satisfaction of knowing you will be remembered." Maybe you will be remembered, for a short time anyway. But do you think that will change anything for you when you are in the grave?

What good does it do, then, to acquire a lot of "stuff" in this life, when you cannot take any of that "stuff" with you when you die? Because you are going to die, acquiring an abundance of things, getting rich, makes no sense. It is meaningless.[1]

Sixth, riches do not solve all of one's problems; they may, in fact, create problems. "Throughout his life [the rich man] also eats in darkness" (5:17). It is interesting, is it not, that Solomon, talking about the rich, says that "he also eats in darkness with great vexation, sickness and anger"? If you want a quiet, peaceful, tranquil life, do not set your mind on becoming rich. With riches come problems. The rich man has worries the poor man does not have. The main worry is: How can I hold onto my riches? What can I do to make sure I keep them? But the rich man must also worry about how to spend those riches. The poor man does not have to choose between buying a thirty-foot yacht or a forty-foot yacht; the rich man does. The poor man does not have to have expensive security systems installed; the rich man does. The poor man does not have to worry about unscrupulous business partners or cheating employees or the likelihood of a recession or how a pandemic will affect the stock market; the rich man does.

In fact, if you think carefully about how many problems go with becoming rich, you might end up saying, "It does not make sense to spend your life trying to get rich!" That is exactly what the author of Ecclesiastes concluded. With riches come vexation, sickness, and anger; therefore, it is stupid to strive for riches. Riches do not give meaning to life.

Seventh, sometimes one who is rich does not get to enjoy his riches. "A man … is given riches and wealth and honor … yet God does not empower him to eat from them" (6:1, 2). Solomon may have had in mind a great king who loses his kingdom to traitorous subjects or one who is defeated by a neighboring country. But the idea can be applied more broadly. Probably we have all heard about rich and famous people who were struck down by disease when they were relatively young. Perhaps even more tragic are those who are rich and famous who literally lose the ability to enjoy their wealth. They may become crippled, or get Alzheimer's or some other debilitating disease, or go blind, or become bedridden with some incurable illness. We feel sorry for them—they have all that money and they cannot enjoy it! They may also feel sorry for them- selves, thinking, "I worked hard, made all that money, and now I cannot make use of it." Whatever the case, if one becomes rich but then cannot use those riches, he is in a pitiful condition. His acquisition of wealth turned out to be in vain.

For all these reasons, Solomon says, living for money is living in vain.

What the New Testament Says About Riches

What does the teaching of Ecclesiastes have to do with us? After all, we live under the New Testament, not the Old.

In fact, the New Testament echoes many of the teachings in Ecclesiastes. It says that riches can keep us from being productive as Christians (Luke 8:14). It says that we are not to lay up for ourselves treasures on earth; rather we are to lay up for ourselves treasures in heaven (Matt 6:19–21). It says that Jesus said that a poor widow who put two small coins into the collection had given more than others who had, they thought, given much more, because, He said, she had put in "all that she had to live on" (Luke 21:1–4). The New Testament indicates that the early Christians were not particularly good at making money, but they were very good at giving it away (Acts 5:34–37, et. al.).

Jesus did *not* say, as some do today, that if you follow Him you will become healthy and wealthy. In fact, He indicated that it would be difficult—though apparently not impossible—for a rich man to enter the kingdom (Matt 19:16–23). The record seems to indicate that though the "common people" heard Jesus gladly, not many rich people came to Him in the first century. Perhaps the best example of Jesus's teaching about the rich and the poor is found in the parable of Lazarus and the rich man. The poor beggar Lazarus ended up in Abraham's bosom; the rich man ended up in the fire of Hades (Luke 16). One who is rich has, in God's sight, no advantage in the kingdom of heaven.

At the same time, the New Testament does *not* teach that someone who is rich cannot be a faithful Christian and ultimately go to heaven! Several passages suggest this idea, but none better than 1 Timothy 6, where Timothy addresses **Christians**:

For the love of money is the root of all sorts of evil, and some by longing for it have wandered away from the faith and pierced themselves with many griefs. But flee from these things, you man of God, and pursue righteousness, godliness, faith, love, perseverance, and gentleness ... . Instruct those who are rich in this present world not to fix their hope on the uncertainty of riches, but on God, who richly supplies us with all things to enjoy. Instruct them to do good, to be rich in good works, to be generous and ready to share, storing up for themselves the treasure of a good foundation for the future, so that they might take hold of that which is life indeed (1 Tim 6:10, 11, 18, 19).

A Christian can be rich and please God if he or she:

1. Does not base his or her hope on those riches (one's riches must be secondary, not primary, in his or her life).
2. Recognizes that everything he or she has comes from God (and is, therefore, both humble and thankful).
3. Uses his or her riches to do good, to engage in good works, and to share with others (doing so is to, as Jesus said, "lay up treasures in heaven").

In other words, a Christian can become rich, but seeking to become rich for the glory and purchasing power that riches result in would be wrong. Furthermore, in Old Testament terms, it would not make for a meaningful life. He who becomes rich for selfish reasons is likely to say at the end of his life: "It was all vanity and striving after wind.

Conclusion

Do we need this message? Think about: What do we spend most of our time doing? Making money and spending it. And what do we value in life? Ask yourself such questions as these:

- What do I value most in life? Is it money, riches, wealth?
- When will I consider myself successful? When I make a lot of money?
- Whom do I consider successful? People who have made a lot of money?
- Whose advice should I follow as I set out in life? Successful, rich people?
- Whom do I admire most? People who have made the most money?
- What do I most look forward to? Making enough money to retire?

• What would make me really happy? Having
  enough money to buy things I want?

It is disturbing, is it not, to consider that some of the
ideas we have believed—perhaps subconsciously—are
not true, and may indicate that we depend too much on
riches? Think about it: Are you depending on the
acquisition of money to make life meaningful? If so,
maybe you should read the book of Ecclesiastes again.

Discussion Questions

1. Discuss: In your opinion, how big a problem
   is the desire for riches in our society today?
   Do you think the problem is worse than it
   was, say, a hundred years ago?
2. Would you agree that "rich" is a relative term
   —that one is defined as "rich" in comparison
   to others—perhaps even others of his own
   class—and therefore cannot be defined by the
   number of dollars one has? For instance, is it
   true that one who had a certain amount of
   money fifty years ago was thought of as
   "rich," but someone with the same amount of
   money today would not be thought of as
   "rich"?
3. How can the Christian find a kind of
   "middle-of-the-road" position between the

extremes of the "health and wealth gospel," on one hand, and the idea that Christians must despise monetary gain, on the other hand? Is it wrong to be rich? Is it wrong to be poor? Under what circumstances would it be right to be rich? To be poor?

4. Jesus told the rich young ruler to sell all he had and give the proceeds to the poor. Is that a message he has for all rich people? Why did he ask it of that one man? Why might it be a good thing for some rich Christians to do today?

5. Where did Jesus say we should "lay up treasures"? Discuss what you think that means.

6. When we think about "riches" or money, perhaps we should also think about how much we give to the church. Are there Christians who are rich but give like they are poor? How should we give?

Endnotes

1. When we talk about dying and what happens after death in this lesson, we are looking at death "under the sun"—that is, at how death looks from a worldly point of view. Looked at from this point of view, the dead are dead and gone and know nothing. They are not

conscious. Their body exists, but it will soon "return to the dust." As Christians, we know "the rest of the story." People live on after they die and are rewarded or punished for how they have lived. In most of Ecclesiastes, Solomon ignores a future eternal existence with God; he is concerned about life and death "under the sun."

6. What About Fame and Power?

What is it that gives life meaning? If it is not work or wisdom, pleasure or riches, then what is it?

Another possibility is fame and power. "If I could just become famous, if I could just become King, or President (or the best-known preacher in the brother-hood), then I would be happy and find self-fulfillment."

The desire for power and fame is understandable. How many little girls have imagined becoming movie stars or doctors? How many little boys have seen themselves as sports heroes or astronauts?

If those dreams come true, if our desire for great-ness is fulfilled, can we be certain we will find life meaningful?

Solomon says, "No."

Solomon's View of Fame and Power

Solomon begins the book of Ecclesiastes by identifying himself as "the son of David, king in Jerusalem" (1:1), and goes on to describe his experience with fame as follows: "Then I became great and increased more than all who preceded me in Jerusalem ... and behold, all was vanity and striving after wind" (2:9a, 11b).

The first thing we need to ask about what Solomon said is: Was Solomon really great? Did he deserve to be called "famous and powerful"?

Note, first, that God promised him glory. When Solomon asked for wisdom, rather than asking for riches and a long life, God said, "I have also given you ... riches and honor, so that there will not be any among the kings like you all your days" (1 Kgs 3:13). If God promised Solomon honor and riches, we would expect him to become powerful and famous.

We learn that is what happened. Solomon became a great king. He ruled over a vast territory. 1 Kings 4:21, 24 says:

> Now Solomon ruled over all the kingdoms from the River to the land of the Philistines and to the border of Egypt; they brought tribute and served Solomon all the days of his life ... . He had dominion over everything west of the River, from Tiphsah even to Gaza, over all the kings west of the River ... .

Solomon ruled over what might be called an empire. It would be hard to dispute the fact that he was powerful.

In addition, Solomon's greatness was evident in his accomplishments—especially in the great works that he built. He said,

> I enlarged my works: I built houses for myself, I planted vineyards for myself; I made gardens and parks for myself and planted in them all kinds of fruit trees; I made ponds of water for myself from which to irrigate a forest of growing trees. (2:4–6)

In addition, Solomon built the large and beautiful temple which took the place of the tabernacle as the center of the worship of the Lord. When you consider the greatness of an earthly ruler, you are likely to ask, "What did he do?" Solomon had good answers to that question.

Solomon became so great that his fame spread throughout that part of the world. For example, he was so famous that the Queen of Sheba[1] heard about him and traveled to Israel to see if he was as powerful and wise as she had heard. When she arrived, she gave him gifts, then tested him with questions, and finally concluded:

I heard in my own land about your words and your wisdom. Nevertheless, I did not believe the reports until I came and my eyes had seen it. And behold, the half was not told me. You exceed in wisdom and prosperity the report which I heard (1 Kgs 10:6b, 7).

Solomon was indeed famous throughout the world, and his fame was well-deserved.

Yet he said that all this was "vanity and striving after wind." Why?

Why Fame and Power are Meaningless

First, making the acquisition of fame and power one's primary goal in life is foolish because fame and power do not last. Solomon does not elaborate on the reason why his greatness did not satisfy his quest for meaning, but he does include one passage which hints at the reason for his conclusion:

A poor but wise lad is better than an old and foolish king who no longer knows how to receive instruction. For he has come out of prison to become king, even though he was born poor in his kingdom. I have seen all the living under the sun throng to the side of the second lad who replaces him. There is no end to all the people, to all who were before him, and even the others who come later will not be happy with him. This too is vanity and striving after wind. (4:13–16)

These verses seem to speak of the vagaries of the monarchy. It describes an old and foolish king who no longer is willing to receive instruction. He is replaced—perhaps forcibly, in a coup—by a "wise lad"—a young man, not a child, not necessarily a teenager—who has come out of prison. This young man becomes king to great acclaim; multitudes "throng to [his] side." But in the end, after all the palace intrigue and changing of monarchs, the multitude, which at first acclaimed the new king, will eventually become disillusioned with him. They "will not be happy with him, for this too is vanity and striving after wind" (4:13–16).[2] The moral of the story? Becoming a king is a vain endeavor because the crowds who at first considered you great will ultimately turn against you. Fame derived from power is fleeting.

Percy Bysshe Shelley, an English poet, wrote a famous sonnet near the beginning of the nineteenth century illustrating that point. Called "Ozymandias," it describes a statue in a distant land, standing by itself in a barren desert. The statue has been mostly destroyed. It now consists of only two stone legs and a dismembered head that has a face with a stern visage, a face of "cold command," on it. The last six lines of the sonnet say:

And on the pedestal these words appear:
"My name is Ozymandias, King of Kings:
Look on my works, ye Mighty, and despair!"
Nothing beside remains. Round the decay
Of that colossal wreck, boundless and bare,
The lone and level sands stretch far away.

According to the poem, Ozymandias thought of himself as "king of kings" and assumed that the evidence of his power would last forever: "Look on my works and despair." He was wrong. After the passage of years, nothing remained of his kingdom! He was not the only ruler to think he had accomplished great things, only to be forgotten, to leave a "wreck" as his legacy, and to be discarded in the desert of man's memory.[3]

And think about this: When Adolph Hitler came to power in Germany in the 1930s, he initiated what he called the "Third Reich," which, according to him, would be a thousand-year reign of his anti-semitic party over Germany (and perhaps over all of Europe). The Second World War followed, Germany was defeated, and Hitler died in 1945. The "thousand-year reign" ended after about ten years. Hitler is remembered for his terrible acts of cruelty, but not for initiating a millennium of Germanic rule.

The fact is: Kingdoms rise and fall, and so do those who rule over them. Whoever depends on achieving power in this life to give meaning to his or her life is headed for disappointment. Power and fame do not last. Those who depend on them to make life meaningful will conclude that life is meaningless—"vanity and striving after wind."

Second, the desire for fame and power is vain because it often leads to sin.

The quest for fame and power can result in sin because it tempts us to seek glory and honor in wrongful ways. We might even question whether the Christian ought to be concerned about achieving power and fame. Jesus said,

> You know that the rulers of the Gentiles lord it over them, and their great men exercise authority over them. It is not this way among you, but whoever wishes to become great among you shall be your servant, and whoever wishes to be first among you shall be your slave; just as the Son of Man did not come to be served, but to serve, and to give His life a ransom for many. (Matt 20:25–28)

He also said, "If anyone wants to be first, he shall be last of all and servant of all" (Luke 9:35). In fact, the desire for fame and power could be the result of "the lust of the flesh and the lust of the eyes and the boastful pride of life" (1 John 2:16). The disciple of Christ should never make gaining glory from men the main aim of his existence.

One problem with seeking and finding prominence and preeminence is that one is tempted to try to achieve fame in sinful, unscrupulous ways. A would-be dictator's thirst for power may lead to attempts to conquer other peoples, murdering and looting and destroying. Others, wanting to be "first," to be seen as "the greatest" or "the best," have lied or stolen to get what they wanted.

Furthermore, seeking fame and power is a meaningless enterprise because it often tempts one who has power to misuse and abuse that power. Ecclesiastes points out that those with power often oppress the powerless (4:1) and speaks of a man "exers[ing] authority over another man to his hurt" (8:9). The person with money and power and fame is often tempted in ways that a poor man is not. A powerful businessman or manufacturer is tempted to abuse his employees. Poor people do not have to worry about mistreating their employees. There is a saying: "Power corrupts, and absolute power corrupts absolutely." That saying is often true.

A biblical example of what the achievement of power can do to someone is provided by the example of the great King David. He had been successful in leading Israel's army to victory over Israel's foes. But when his kingdom was firmly established, in the spring of the year "when kings go out to battle" (1 Kgs 11:1). David stayed in his palace enjoying his leisure. Then—because he had achieved power—he took Bathsheba and committed adultery with her. If he had not been powerful, probably he would not have been tempted to do what he did. Solomon may be another example. At the first of his reign, he had God's full approval. But he was tempted, and gave in to temptation, to take many wives—including foreign, idol-worshiping wives. The result was that he was guilty of idolatry. Without his fame and power, he would not have been able to have all those foreign wives!

It would probably be the same with us. The more power, the more fame, we have, the more ways we are likely to be tempted, and the stronger the temptation is likely to be, and the more likely we are to succumb to it.

In addition, the desire for glory and honor is wrong because it often causes us to think that we—in and of ourselves—are responsible for our success. The Bible says that "every good gift and every perfect gift is from above" (Jas 1:17, KJV). Thus, whatever power or glory one receives in this world is the result of what God has given him. Paul indicated that those who rule over a country receive their authority from God and that they are "ministers of God" and "servants of God" (Rom 13:1–8).

God providentially puts into power, or allows to be put into power, whomever he chooses. Therefore, the king or government authority, whoever he is, has no reason to be proud; he has nothing to boast about.

But the acquisition of power tends to cause princes and kings—and maybe senators and presidents—to forget where their power came from—namely, from God.

One example is provided by the New Testament. In Acts 12:21–23 we read:

> On an appointed day Herod, having put on his royal apparel, took his seat on the rostrum and began delivering an address to them. The people kept crying out, "The voice of a god and not of a man!" And immediately an angel of the Lord struck him because he did not give God the glory and he was eaten by worms and died.

Another example is found in the book of Daniel. Powerful people today may be like the Babylonian king Nebuchadnezzar, whose kingdom had just been established when the following happened:

> The king reflected and said, "Is this not Babylon the great, which I myself have built as a royal residence by the might of my power and for the glory of my majesty?" While the word was still in the king's mouth, a voice came from heaven, saying, "King Nebuchadnezzar, to you it is declared: sovereignty

has been removed from you ... [until] you recognize
that the Most High is ruler over the realm of
mankind and bestows it on whomever He wishes."
(Dan 4:30–32)

In like manner, once we have achieved fame and
power we are likely to think: "Look what I did! Honor
me for my achievements! I am the greatest!" At the
same time, we lose sight of the fact that, wherever we
are, no matter how high in government or business or
education we find ourselves, God put us there! To fail
to acknowledge God as the One who gave us our fame
and power is to sin—and if our desire to be famous and
powerful leads us to sin, it makes our life, at best,
meaningless.

Conclusion

No doubt about it: He who makes fame and power his
primary goal will ultimately discover that his quest is
"vain and striving after wind."

However, the Bible does not teach that it is wrong to
be either famous or powerful. Though most New
Testament Christians were poor, some were rich and
some occupied positions of authority. King David
(though he sinned) was a "man after God's own heart."
You have probably known people (as I have) who had
achieved a measure of fame, or who were regarded as

powerful—perhaps government officials—who remained faithful Christians, giving God the glory, and who were seeking to advance the cause of Christ with all their hearts. Imagine the good that could be done by a star NBA player who was also a faithful Christian who attributed his success to the Lord and wanted, more than anything else, to see others saved and the church built up!

Therefore from God's standpoint, the question is not just "Are you powerful or famous?" Rather, the Christian should ask himself four questions:

1. Have I made power and fame my primary objectives in life? If so, you will find that your life is "vain and striving after wind."
2. Do I take credit for the power or fame I enjoy? Or do I give God the glory? Are you proud and self-centered, or humble and thankful, acknowledging that whatever your accomplishments, the glory belongs to God?
3. How have I chosen to use whatever fame and power I have? To do good? To bring glory to God? Or to enhance my lifestyle and garner glory for myself?
4. Has my major aim in life been to be glorified and served by others, or has it been to serve others?

One final word: The person who seeks fame and power can legitimately find it after this life is over. He can receive the "crown of life"! (Rev 2:10; see the context for other promises) If you really want fame and power, plan to go to heaven, and do what is necessary to get there—what is necessary to become a Christian and then to live as a faithful Christian!

Discussion Questions

1. Do you agree that "fame and power do not last"? Can you think of examples which either prove or disprove this point? When we apply this fact to ourselves, should it make a difference? Do we not all want to be remembered? To "leave a name for ourselves"? Is that not a natural tendency? Is there anything wrong with it? What's the problem then? (Is it: There's nothing wrong with wanting to be remembered, but if you live only for that, you will be disappointed.)

2. How will you be remembered? For what will you be remembered? It's a question worth considering.

3. With fame and power, as with riches, if acquiring them is your main aim in life, even if you succeed, do you think you will be completely satisfied?

4. It might also be worth considering: Is there a "downside" to become famous in this world? Would you then become the object of sometimes unwelcome attention by others?

5. Discuss: Is the desire for fame and power inherently wrong? Without it, would the human race be better off? If it is inherently bad, then why did God promise us a "crown of life" as an incentive to be "faithful unto death"? If it is not inherently wrong, when does it become wrong?

Endnotes

1. "Sheba" is said to be Yemen in *Eerdmans' Handbook to the Bible*. David Alexander and Pat Alexander, eds., *Eerdmans' Handbook to the Bible* (Grand Rapids, MI: Eerdmans, 1973), 258.

2. This is approximately the interpretation preferred by: Michael A. Eaton, *Ecclesiastes*, Tyndale Old Testament Commentaries. (Downers Grove, IL: Inter-Varsity Press, 1983), 95–97.

3. The pyramids of Egypt, mentioned earlier in these lessons, provide another example. Everyone knows there are pyramids which were intended to immortalize their builders, but almost no one knows the names of the builders.

7. What About Evil and Injustice?

The book of Ecclesiastes asserts that "all is vanity and striving after wind." Life is meaningless or vain. Why? Because the things we spend our lives seeking disappoint us. For example, even if we find them—even if we acquire wisdom, fame, power, and riche—even if we work hard and accomplish great things—even if we live lives of unending pleasure—our lives will ultimately prove to be "striving after wind" because nothing lasts. Everything we accomplish will eventually be forgotten.

But life is also meaningless—"vanity" and "striving after wind"—because evil abounds and injustice prevails. And where evil abounds and injustice prevails, life—even for those who are not evil and not purposely unfair—seems futile, meaningless, vain.

Let us consider the things that Solomon says make life on this planet, under the sun, evil and unfair.

Evil Abounds

A good person seeking a life with meaning wants to live in a good world—a world in which most people do good, in which a clear distinction is made between good and evil, and in which evil people are punished and good people are rewarded. A world that is different —where the line between good and evil is unclear and where evil people are likely to go unpunished—a world in which evil seems to be more common than good—is strange, unnerving, uncomfortable. Observing it, one who is seeking meaning in life, might end up saying, "Life is meaningless. If there is going to be so much evil, and if evil deeds go unpunished, what is the point of living?" That was Solomon's reaction to the world in which he lived. He found a number of things wrong with his world.

People Are Sinful. Solomon considered those about him and concluded that men are sinful. He said, "Behold, I have found only this, that God made men upright, but they have sought out many devices" (7:29). In 9:3 Solomon wrote, "The hearts of the sons of men are full of evil." Furthermore, he observed life and concluded:

I have seen under the sun that in the place of justice there is wickedness and in the place of righteousness there is wickedness. I said to myself, "God will judge both the righteous man and the wicked man," for a time for every matter and every deed is there (3:16, 17).

Solomon notes what the original state of man was. When God first created him, he was sinless; Genesis says this created being was "very good." But the first man sinned, and all others have followed in his steps. All have sinned. Is life worth living, Solomon wonders, in a world in which sin, or wickedness, is so prevalent?

The Poor Are Oppressed. The prevalence of sin is also obvious in the fact that men wickedly take advantage of one another. Ecclesiastes says, "If you see oppression of the poor and denial of justice and righteousness in the province, do not be shocked at the sight" (5:8a). He gives an example in the previous chapter:

Then I looked again at all the acts of oppression that were being done under the sun. And behold I saw the tears of the oppressed and they had no one to comfort them, and on the side of the oppressors was power, but they had no one to comfort them. So I congratulated the dead who are already dead more than the living who are still living. But better off than both of them is the one who has never existed, who has never seen the evil activity that is done under the sun (4:1–3).

"What is the use of living?" Solomon asks, "in a world that is so evil, in which the oppressed can find no relief?" We may exhibit a similar attitude today. Did you ever hear anyone say, "I hope I never live to see the day when . . ." Then he or see will add some extraordinarily sinful act. Chances are, he or she will in fact live to see the day, and will feel much like Solomon did: "I had just as soon have died as to see such a terrible thing happen."

Even Good Things Are the Consequence of Evil Motives. Solomon wrote, "I have seen that every labor and every skill which is done is the result of rivalry between a man and his neighbor. This too is vanity and striving after wind" (4:4). It would be nice if people used their talents for good. Instead, they use the talents God has given them to put down their neighbors, to shame them, to get the better of them. We live in a wicked world indeed, Solomon seems to be saying, when even the good things that happen result from sinful desires.

People Deliberately and Maliciously Hurt One Another. Solomon adds, "All this I have seen and applied my mind to every deed that has been done under the sun wherein a man has exercised authority over another man to his hurt" (8:9). The "survival of the fittest" mentality, the "dog eat dog" philosophy, may be all right for the animal kingdom, but people are supposed to be better than that! So it is a shame, Solomon says, when one man can take advantage of another, even hurt the other, and get away with it! If that happens, we live in an upside-down society. In fact, life is hardly worth living. It is vain!

Think of it like this: Suppose you love beauty—everyone does—and you want the yard around your house to be beautiful. Consequently you plant grass and flowers and engage in hours of backbreaking labor to try to make your lawn beautiful. But the lawn will grow nothing but weeds, tall weeds, ugly weeds, that mar the beauty, not only of your house but also of the whole countryside! How would you feel? Maybe you would feel: "If life is like this, if there's no beauty to be found, and I can do nothing about it, I had just as soon not be alive!" That is the way Solomon felt about the overwhelming sinfulness of the world!

Injustice Prevails

Life's meaninglessness derives not only from the evil that abounds on this planet, but also from the fact that life is often unfair. Injustice prevails. Solomon uses a number of examples to illustrate this point.

People's Desires Are Not Satisfied. Solomon writes,

If a man fathers a hundred children and lives many years, however many they be, but his soul is not satisfied with good things and he does not even have a proper burial, then I say, "Better the miscarriage than he, for it comes in futility and goes into obscurity; and its name is covered in obscurity. It never sees the sun and it never knows anything; it is better off than he. Even if the other man lives a thousand years twice and does not enjoy good things—do not all go to one place?" (6:3–6)

What is the problem with the man pictured in this description? "His soul is not satisfied," says Solomon. Apparently he does well financially, but still "his soul is not satisfied"—he never gets enough. Therefore, he is miserable. Besides that, he "does not have a proper burial," so, presumably, he is not appreciated by his family or community. If he cannot find satisfaction even from a successful career, and if he cannot find respect in his community, he might as well be dead, Solomon says!

Sometimes Those Who Deserve to Succeed Do Not Do So. Solomon says,

I saw again under the sun that the race is not to the swift and the battle is not to the warriors, and neither bread to the wise or wealth to the discerning nor favor to men of ability, for time and chance overtake us all (9:11).

An interesting thought! But we know its truth. Sometimes, for one of a number of reasons, the better or best athlete does not win the contest; the smartest kid is not named the valedictorian; the most gifted writer does not win the prize. And sometimes, by some fluke, the less well-trained, less well-equipped army wins the battle over better troops. When any of these things happen, we wonder "how" or "why"... And then we are likely to conclude: Life just is not fair. Its unfairness—especially if we are the ones who should have won but did not—may then lead us to say with Solomon: "It is all meaningless—vanity and striving after wind."

Good Deeds Are Forgotten. When you go out of your way to help someone or to do some other good deed, you expect your kindness to be remembered. You do not expect to be paid, but you do expect those who were helped to remember you with thankfulness. The fact is: Sometimes they do not. Solomon cited such a case:

> Also this I came to see as wisdom under the sun, and it impressed me. There was a small city with few men in it and a great king came to it, surrounded it and constructed large siegeworks against it. But there was

found in it a poor wise man and he delivered the city by his wisdom. Yet no one remembered that poor man. So I said, "Wisdom is better than strength." But the wisdom of the poor man is despised and his words are not heeded (9:13–16).

"But no one remembered that poor man" who had saved the city! How do you think he felt? How would you have felt? Have you ever done something good, accomplished something significant that benefitted other people, only to be forgotten? How did you feel? Maybe you felt like Solomon: Life is not worth living. It is meaningless—"vanity and striving after wind."

The Wicked Are Rewarded and the Righteous Are Punished. Sometimes life seems meaningless because the rewards people receive for their actions are unfair. Solomon wrote, "I have seen everything during my lifetime of futility; there is a righteous man who perishes in his righteousness and there is a wicked man who prolongs his life in his wickedness" (7:15). He also said,

There is futility which is done on the earth, that is, there are righteous men to whom it happens according to the deeds of the wicked. On the other hand, there are evil men to whom it happens according to the deeds of the righteous. I say that this too is futility (8:14).

What should happen when one is wicked? He should be punished, right? What should happen when a man is righteous? He should be rewarded with good things, right? Solomon says that is not how it often happens. The righteous are punished, and the wicked are rewarded! It would be like spanking the good child because he politely said, "Thank you," and giving a candy bar to the bad child because he slapped his little brother.

Does that kind of thing happen? Are all righteous people rich? Are all wicked people poor? We know that oft the wicked prosper and the righteous suffer. And we know it is not fair. And if we think about it, we probably agree that when it happens it makes life meaningless.

People Do Not Learn from the Punishment of Evil. Solomon wrote,

> So then, I have seen the wicked buried, who used to go in and out from the holy place, and they are soon forgotten in the city where they did thus. This too is futility. Because the sentence against an evil deed is not executed quickly, therefore the hearts of the sons of men among them are fully given to evil (8:10, 11).

Apparently the point of this passage is that others are supposed to learn from the punishment that is meted out to the guilty. A wicked man is buried; he is well known—he went in and out of the city—; but he is forgotten—presumably his evil deeds and their consequences are forgotten. Thus, no one learns from his life and death. Furthermore, if he is not punished soon after he committed a crime, no one will learn from his execution. Thus, even when evil is recognized and evildoers are punished, their punishment does not necessarily have the desired effect. People forget it and are not changed by it. Again, such facts are frustrating and keep life from having meaning.

Incompetent People Are Honored and Competent People Are Forgotten. In 10:6, 7 we read, "Folly is set in many exalted places while rich men sit in humble places. I have seen slaves riding on horses and princes walking like slaves in the land." Solomon's assumption is that rich men and princes are more competent and worthy of respect than foolish men and slaves, so it is strange—and unjust—when those who are less competent are honored and those who are more competent are not recognized for their abilities and achievements. Again, I suspect that most of us have seen what we would think of as the equivalent: Competent intelligent people overlooked when jobs are handed out or honors are awarded, while less competent people (perhaps related to the boss or the judge) get the job or the awards. This, too, says Solomon, makes life meaningless.

Accidents Happen, Even to Hardworking People. In 10:8, 9 we find this interesting passage: "He who digs a pit may fall into it, and a serpent may bite him who breaks through a wall. He who quarries stones may be hurt by them, and he who splits logs may be endangered by them." The tragedy of accidents happening to the innocent is compounded by the fact that the people to whom the accidents happen are hardworking men—people who dig ditches and quarry stones and split wood.

We can all identify with such incidents. Accidents happen to all of us. We may have the best of intentions; we may even be careful; we may do the best we can to be safe—and we may still be hurt by an accident. It seems unfair. Such unfairness seems to contribute to the view that life is vain.

Conclusion

To conclude: Solomon, in various places in Ecclesiastes, says that "all is vanity" because evil abounds and injustice prevails. We might be inclined to disagree with that conclusion. For instance, how many of us when we were little, and something disagreeable happened—maybe an older brother or sister received privileges we did not have—have complained to our parents, "That's not fair!" Only to be told by our parents: "Life is not fair!" The point was: We should not expect life to be fair! Likewise, we live in a fallen, sinful world. Why should we expect anything else but to see evil abound? Why then should unfairness and wrongdoing lead anyone to conclude that "all is vanity"?

In reply: Remember that Ecclesiastes presents life "under the sun," life on earth as it is, not life as it ought to be, and not life beyond the grave. Solomon then is talking about how he feels when he observes life "under the sun." He sees the evil and unfairness of life and he feels: "Life is vain!"

If we talk to our children, or to one another, we can truthfully say, "The evil and injustice in the world do not mean that life is meaningless!" But saying it and believing it, or acting as if you believe it, are two different things. Seeing unfairness and evil can make us feel as if life is meaningless.

How we feel is important. Feelings may not reflect reality, but feelings are real. They are a reality that must be dealt with. When we feel so disappointed, so discouraged, so unhappy, that we feel life is meaningless, our feelings are important. Injustice and evil do not make life meaningless, but if you feel that they do, they might as well.

Is there any Christian response to such feelings? The New Testament teaches Christians to expect suffering, and even to expect to be persecuted, and they can take comfort from the fact that "all things work together for good" (Rom 8:28). The abundance of evil should not surprise the Christian. We know that all have sinned (Rom 3:23) and that sin reigns in this present world.

Our difference with the view of Ecclesiastes is that we know we can gain forgiveness for our sins and we can teach the gospel to others so that they can be saved from their sins. Christians know—though they might find it hard to believe in difficult circumstances—that the abundance of evil and the fact of unfairness do not make life meaningless.

As far as fairness is concerned, one further point needs to be made. The one time when absolute fairness will be obvious will be on the Day of Judgment. On that day every person will receive according to what he or she has done, whether good or bad. God will do the judging, and He will make no mistakes! You do not need to worry about that judgment being unfair!

And that leads to this question: On that day, when you are perfectly judged, will you be rewarded for righteousness or punished for unforgiven sins?

Discussion Questions

1. Can you think of examples of evil and/or injustice today—maybe even examples that illustrate the points Solomon makes? Can you think of examples of injustice that affect, or have affected, you? Would you agree that we live in a world in which "evil (often)

abounds" and "injustice (frequently) prevails?
Is it possible for us to feel today that life is
meaningless because of all the evil and
injustice we see about us?

2. How, according to the New Testament,
   should the Christian personally react to evil
   and injustice? Can you cite New Testament
   passages to prove your point?

3. Should the Christian himself or herself ever
   engage in evil or unjust acts? If he or she
   does, can he or she be forgiven? What does he
   or she need to do to be forgiven?

4. Although the Bible does not permit the
   Christian to strike back, or seek revenge, for
   acts of evil or injustice he or she personally
   experiences, is anything wrong with a
   Christian working within the law to try to
   make society better—a place where there is
   less evil and less injustice? How might he or
   she do so?

8. What About Death?

The primary point of the book of Ecclesiastes is that life is vain, or meaningless. What makes it that way? We might think otherwise, but Solomon seems to say that the main thing that subtracts meaning from living is dying! Solomon says the fact of death—the fact that we must all die—makes life "vain and striving after wind."

For example, he says that "there is no lasting remembrance of the wise man as with the fool, inasmuch as in the coming days all will be forgotten. And how the wise man and the fool alike die!" (2:16) No matter what you have done here, it will be forgotten because you will die.

Again, according to 2:18, 19, Solomon hated all his labor because he would have to leave everything to someone else when he died, but, he said, "who knows" whether that man "will be a wise man or a fool." He expected to die, and that made him say his labor had been in vain.

Then in 5:15, 16, he wrote:

As he had come naked from his mother's womb, so will he return as he came. He will take nothing from the fruit of his labor that he can carry in his hand. This also is a grievous evil—exactly as a man is born, thus will he die. So what is the advantage to him who toils for the wind?

When death comes, says Solomon, you can take none of the things you have worked for with you into the grave. That means you were toiling "for the wind." Your work, your life, was meaningless because of the nature of the death that ended it.

No doubt Solomon felt that death made life "vain and striving after wind." Let us consider specific facts about death that, according to Solomon, make life meaningless.

Solomon's View of Death

Solomon says . . .

The Death of Human Beings Is Like That of Animals.

Humans like to think of themselves as superior to animals, so it comes as a shock to hear Solomon say:

> I said to myself concerning the sons of men, "God has surely tested them in order for them to see that they are but beasts." For the fate of the sons of men and the fate of beasts is the same. As one dies so dies the other; indeed, they all have the same breath, and there is no advantage for man over beast, for all is vanity. All go to the same place. All came from the dust and all return to the dust. Who knows that the breath of man ascends upward and the breath of the beast descends downward to the earth? (3:18–21)

What is Solomon saying? He is talking about life "under the sun"—about life as we experience it here on this planet without any consideration of what we might call spiritual truths. When we look at life that way, there appears to be—as far as life and death are concerned—no significant difference between man and animals. Both are made up of the same kind of physical matter, so when they die their bodies experience the same kind of decay. If a dog dies and a human dies, both, from a worldly standpoint, have the same experience and end up in the same place—united with the dust from which they came.

From that fact, Solomon draws the conclusion that

life is vain. You can understand why. I can imagine someone saying, "I'm no better than the animals? I'm just an animal myself? If that's the case, what's the use of living? What's the good of anything?" That is the point that Solomon is making.

We need to be careful in applying these verses. Some might like to use them to prove that man has no soul, no spirit that lives on after death, that humans are like the "old dog Rover—when they are dead, they are dead all over!"

If this were the only passage in the Bible that dealt with the subject of life after death, one might be justified in reaching that conclusion (even though Solomon opens the door to the possibility of continuing life for humans when he says "who knows" whether man ascends). But this is not the only passage in the Bible that discusses that subject.

In the story of creation, a distinction is made between man and animals. Man became a "living soul" and was made in the image of God and given dominion over the animals and the rest of creation. Solomon says that when a man dies, "The dust will return to the earth as it was, and the spirit will return to God who gave it" (12:7).

In the New Testament the story of Lazarus and the rich man (Luke 16) gives evidence that people live on after death, as does the fact that Jesus on the cross said to the thief, "Today you will be with me in Paradise," not "Today you will completely go out of existence." And the book of Revelation pictures Christian martyrs praising God around His throne (Rev 6). When Paul, in Philippians 1, speaks of death he says it is better to die than to live because dying means we depart to be with Christ.

The Bible must be understood as a whole: Just because Solomon, writing about what life looks like "under the sun," does not mention life after death does not prove that there is no life after death.

Everyone Dies. A second fact about death presented in Ecclesiastes is that everyone must die (with the exception—we learn in the New Testament—of those who are still living when Christ returns). You cannot escape death by being good or doing good. The righteous and the wicked, the good and the evil—all alike die. Here is the way Solomon put it:

> For I have taken all this to my heart and explain it that righteous men, wise men, and their deeds are in the hand of God. Man does not know whether it will be love or hatred; anything awaits him. It is the same for all. There is one fate for the righteous and for the wicked; for the good, for the clean and for the unclean; for the man who offers a sacrifice and the one who does not sacrifice. As the good man is, so is

the sinner; as the swearer is, so is the one who is afraid to swear. This is an evil in all that is done under the sun, that there is one fate for all men. Furthermore, the hearts of the sons of men are full of evil and insanity is in their hearts throughout their lives. Afterwards they go to the dead (9:1–3).

Should a righteous man be rewarded with life, while a wicked man is punished with death? Our common sense says so, as does our understanding of God's mercy and God's wrath. But is that what always happens? Not always. Sometimes evil people live a long time, and righteous people are cut down in their prime. How is that fair?

Solomon is saying that the fact that one fate comes to all—good and bad, righteous and wicked, lawkeepers and lawbreakers—makes life meaningless, vain, "striving after wind." Why be good if you die just like the person who is wicked? And what is the point of living if there is no difference between the death of the righteous and the death of the wicked?

Life Is Better Than Death. Solomon also makes the rather obvious point that life is to be preferred to death. Anyone who is alive, therefore, is better off than anyone who has died.

For whoever is joined with all the living, there is hope; surely a live dog is better than a dead lion. For the living know they will die; but the dead do not know anything, nor have they any longer a reward, for their memory is forgotten. Indeed their love, their hate and their zeal have already perished and they will no longer have a share in all that is done under the sun (9:4–6).

The point of these verses is obvious: to present the truth that life is better than death (at least if we are thinking only of life "under the sun," without considering afterlife consequences). No one, therefore, should choose to die.

How this thought fits into the context of Ecclesiastes is not so clear. Perhaps Solomon expected someone reading the book to conclude, "If life is so meaningless, I might as well end it all." Solomon therefore may be saying, "Even if life seems bleak and drear and disappointing, even if you can see no point to living, it is still better to be alive than dead." Maybe Solomon is saying that life does not become less meaningless if we end our own lives.

We, too, need to be convinced that, no matter how bad things are, no matter how vain and meaningless life seems to be, it is better to be alive than dead. "A live dog is better than a dead lion."

No One Can Control Death. Ecclesiastes 8:8 says, "No man has the authority to restrain the wind with the wind, or authority over the day of death; and there is no discharge in the time of war, and evil will not deliver those who practice it." We have no more authority over death than we do over the wind. Just as we cannot stop the wind from blowing by ordering it do so, neither can we prevent death, when it comes upon us, from ending our lives.

Yes, we may be able to postpone death with good health habits and medical treatment. But we have all seen people who we thought were going to die recover. And we have all seen people who seemed to be doing well physically die suddenly and unexpectedly. Such things happen so often that there is a saying to describe it: "If it's your time to go, you'll die. If not, you won't." I am not sure whether that view is either logical or scriptural, but the point is that the unexpected happens so often that people feel justified in saying it.

Therefore, we can think of it like this: Death is like a hungry predator—perhaps a large, fierce tiger—prowling around looking for a victim to destroy and devour. If his eyes fall on you, you can do nothing to prevent him from killing you! That is what is frustrating! There is no real protection from death once it gets us in its crosshairs. We cannot protect ourselves. We have no authority over it. And that is another reason why death makes life "vanity and striving after wind."

Finally, Death Makes Life Meaningless Because It Is Often Preceded by a Painful Old Age. In chapter twelve, as Solomon reaches the conclusion of the book, he uses a series of metaphors to describe what often happens when people get old. People cannot see as well; their hands shake; their back and legs give way so that they stoop or are bent over when they stand; they lose most of their teeth; they experience irrational fears; they cannot hear as well as they did; they get up unnecessarily early every day; they lose their sexual desire (12:2–5). No wonder they say of those days, "I have no delight in them" (12:1). Death is then described as the breaking of a silver cord, the crushing of a golden bowl, the shattering of a pitcher, and the crushing of a wheel at the cistern (12:6). The fact that such travail precedes death makes life meaningless: "'Vanity of vanities,' says the Preacher, 'all is vanity'" (12:8).

The New Testament View of Death

Of course, Christians have a more accurate view of death than Solomon's impressions expressed in Ecclesiastes. Let us summarize some of what the New Testament teaches about death:

Death is universal. "It is appointed for men to die once. After this comes judgment" (Heb 9:27). Everyone dies. (With the exception of those who are still alive when Christ returns; see 1 Cor 15:51.)

Death is our enemy (1 Cor 15:26). It is an enemy because it is the consequence of sin. The devil possesses the "power of death" (Heb 2:14). Ultimately, the second coming of Christ will destroy the enemy death.

Death is the separation of the soul or spirit from the body (Jas 2:26). When the spirit or soul leaves, the body dies.

Human beings die spiritually when they sin in the sense that they are separated from God and the spiritual blessings He provides (Rom 6:23). Jesus's death rescues those who are dead in sin and makes them alive again (Eph 2:1–5).

Christians who die are welcomed into the presence of the Lord (Phil 1:23; see also Luke 16:22). Therefore, those who "die in the Lord" are blessed (Rev 14:13).

Someday when Christ returns there will be a resurrection from the dead of both the good and the bad (John 5:28, 29). The judgment of all will follow, and the results of that judgment will be that individuals will be either welcomed into heaven or be consigned to hell—for an eternity.

Our View of Death

We probably know and believe what the New Testament teaches about death. We can take comfort in the fact that our book, the New Testament, teaches us more about life after death than the Old Testament taught the Jews. The Old Testament suggested the possibility of life after death and of a resurrection (Ps 23 says, for instance, "I will dwell in the house of the Lord forever"), but it did not clearly teach what the New Testament makes plain to its readers.

Therefore, we can know, and most of us do know, the facts about death—including the fact that death is not the end, that resurrection follows, and that heaven awaits the faithful. We should be thankful that God has revealed these facts to us.

Does knowing these facts mean that we are no longer plagued with a negative view of death—that death does not, at least to some degree, at some time, make life seem meaningless? We know that everyone dies, that the death of a human being is similar to the death of an animal, that we have no control over death, that life is better than death, and that many problems often curse the lives of older people before they pass away. Thus, in spite of the fact that our brain knows better, our feelings may make us feel that death makes life vain, nothing more than striving after wind.

For example, as we anticipate our own death we may look back on our lives and wonder whether we really accomplished anything, and we may look forward to a life of pain and suffering before we die—and we may be tempted to think, "What's the use? Life has no meaning anyway."

Or we may lose a loved one and experience similar feelings. I recently lost my wife of sixty-two years. It is hard to know how to describe my feelings since then. She was my friend, my lover, my co-worker. We worked together, played together, ate together, traveled together, worshiped together—for sixty-two years! I find it hard to get up in the morning and harder to go to bed at night because she is not here. I constantly feel I have something I need to tell somebody—a bit of gossip, a creative thought, a crazy opinion—but I have no one to tell it to. I used to bring her hot tea at night; now I have no one to take hot tea to. We have a decorative pillow on our bed with the words "Love You More" on it. We used to pick up that pillow, throw it around, and pretend to fight as we said, in turn, "I love you more!" "No, I love you more!" Our "fight" always ended in a cuddle and a kiss. No more.

I have no doubt that heaven awaits my departed wife. She was a faithful Christian for more than sixty years. But that does not keep me from feeling miserable about her going on without me. Sometimes I wonder: Without Sharlotte, what's the use? Why should I live? Life seems meaningless—"vanity and striving after wind." I know what Solomon means when he says that death makes life seem meaningless.

Conclusion

When faced with our feelings about death, what should we do? The solution is not to refuse to mourn for one we have lost. We do not mourn as do those who have no faith and no hope (1 Thess 4:13), but we do mourn when we lose a loved one. "Jesus wept" (John 10:35) at the grave of Lazarus; when they buried Stephen, the disciples made "loud lamentation" over him (Acts 8:2); similarly, the church mourned the passing of Dorcas (Acts 9:39); Christians are told to "weep with those who weep" (Rom 12:15). Why mourn if we believe that one who died will live again and be blessed? For many reasons: We miss them; we miss the good that they did; their death leaves a hole in our lives or in the life of the family, the church, the business, or the nation; we loved them and love does not want to turn loose.

There is, therefore, no reason for the Christian not to mourn when a loved one dies. Maybe we could even say that there is nothing wrong with feeling that life has lost its meaning at such times.

However, even when we mourn, we must not lose sight of the facts that are implanted in our brains. One of those facts is that someone who dies in Christ is better off than when he or she lived. That fact can somewhat ease our pain, provide us with comfort and hope, and give life meaning.

Maybe the most important thing we need to learn about death is this: It is coming to us all. It is coming to you, as well as to me. And after death comes judgment. We will be judged, not primarily on what we know, but on what we do. One who is a faithful Christian can—though it is not likely that he or she will—actually look forward to death, the judgment, and eternity; being a faithful child of God therefore gives meaning to life, in spite of the fact of death.

In contrast, one who is not a faithful Christian can never look forward to dying.

The question is: Can you?

Discussion Questions

1. The main point made by Solomon regarding death is that, because it brings life to an end, it makes life meaningless or vain. Discuss this idea. Make sure you understand what Solomon is saying. Do you agree or disagree, and why?

2. The Christian view of death is obviously very different from that presented by Solomon because it takes into account the eternal consequences of our life on earth. Nevertheless, when we think about the smashed hopes and broken dreams and unfinished business that death often results in, is it possible for even Christians to see Solomon's point and agree with it?

3. What should we do—how should we live—to prepare for our own inevitable death? What can we do in life to make our death less difficult for our family and friends? Is it really possible for Christians, when a brother

or sister in Christ dies, not to mourn as
others mourn?

4. What experience have you had in connection
   with the death of a loved one? How did you
   feel? As a result of your loved one's death, did
   life seem empty? Meaningless? Is it possible
   to feel that way even if only Christians are
   involved?

9. If Life Is Meaningless, How Should We Live?

I f life is so dismal, so bleak … if all is meaningless, "vanity," "striving after wind" … what should we do? How should we live?

Should We Quit Living? Answer: No, Suicide is Not an Option

In our present age one might respond: "If life is meaningless, why go on living? Let us just kill ourselves and get it over with." Given the number of suicides in our society, to some it might seem reasonable—if one is faced with a meaningless existence—to kill oneself and end the suffering.

However, the writer of Ecclesiastes never suggests suicide as a solution to the problem of meaninglessness. He says it would be better not to have been born than to live such a meaningless life, but he never says it would be better to kill yourself than to live.

In fact, only a few suicides are recorded in the whole Bible.[1] People then did not feel free to kill themselves if things did not go their way. Why? I suppose suicide was not seen as an option because the people believed that men were made "in the image of God" and were given life by God Himself and therefore they had no right to take their own lives—to kill, or murder, someone valued by God whose life came from God. That is an attitude all of us need today.

Then How Should We Live? Answer: Make the Best of a Bad Situation

If not suicide, then what? How should one respond to an almost helpless and hopeless situation? The book of Ecclesiastes answers that question. Its theme is that life has no meaning. Yet it gives some detailed instructions about how we should live. How can you explain that? If life is meaningless, why do you need to worry about how you live?

Here is my answer: Our situation is somewhat similar to that of a criminal sentenced to life in prison. When he arrives at the penitentiary, what should he do? What advice would you give him? "Live any way you want." "Be rebellious; they cannot punish you any more than they have already. If you want to steal or hurt people or even kill someone, go ahead." "Do nothing; you will not get into trouble then."

If you were the criminal's friend, you would have better advice for him. You would advise him: "You are in prison to stay for the rest of your life. It is not a happy situation. But you are stuck there, so you might as well make the best of it. Follow the rules, be respectful, be helpful, find something to do that will be enjoyable, and you will find that life will be much better for you. Even though you are in jail, you can make the best of your bad situation by living the best life possible."

Similarly, we have been "sentenced" to serve a lifetime on this planet, "under the sun," living what is, or seems to be, a meaningless existence. What should we do about it? The answer: Make the most of a bad situation. Even though life (apart from God) is, in the long run, meaningless, live as you should and you will lead a much better, more enjoyable life, even if at the end of it you have to say, "All is vanity."

In other words, life may be long and tedious and meaningless, but there are some rules which, if we follow them, will make life less tedious, which will help us enjoy our time spent "under the sun."

How Can You Make the Most of Your Bad Situation? Answer: Enjoy Life!

What should we do since we are "imprisoned" in a meaningless life? God offers human beings "imprisoned" on this earth this advice: Enjoy yourself!

That sounds strange. Does God want us to enjoy life when He tells us "all is vanity and striving after wind"?

Some might think that good people, Christians for instance, should be grave, serious, solemn. After all, as a poet said, "Life is real, life is earnest, and the grave is not the goal." When life lacks meaning, is there any reason to be happy? Should we not spend our time with sober faces, thinking constantly about the problems that we face?

Should we really enjoy life? Surely God does not expect us to experience joy in a meaningless universe. To answer that question, consider the following passages from the book of Ecclesiastes (quoted from the RSV):

- There is nothing better for a man than that he should eat and drink and find enjoyment in his toil. This also, I saw, is from the hand of God; for apart from him who can eat or who can have enjoyment? (2:24, 25)
- I know there is nothing better for them than to be happy and enjoy themselves as long as

they live; also that it is God's gift to man that everyone should eat and drink and take pleasure in all his toil (3:12,13).

- So I saw that there is nothing better than that a man should enjoy his work, for that is his lot; who can bring him to see what will be after him? (3:22)
- Behold, what I have seen to be good and to be fitting is to eat and drink and find enjoyment in all the toil with which one toils under the sun the few days of his life which God has given him, for this is his lot (5:18; see also 5:19,20).
- I commend enjoyment, for man has no good thing under the sun but to eat, and drink, and enjoy himself, for this will go with him in his toil through the days of life which God gives him under the sun (8:15).
- Go, eat your bread with enjoyment, and drink your wine with a merry heart ... let your garments be always white; let not oil be lacking on your head. Enjoy life with the wife whom you love, all the days of your vain life which he has given you under the sun, because that is your portion in life ... whatever your hand finds to do, do it with your might ... (9:7,10).
- Bread is made for laughter, and wine

gladdens life, and money answers everything (10:19).

- Indeed, if a man should live many years, let him rejoice in them all; but let him remember that the days of darkness will be many. All that comes is vanity (11:7,8).

All these passages teach us that, even though life is serious and living can be tedious and everything seems to be meaningless, God wants us to enjoy life.

In fact, God made us and placed us on this planet to find enjoyment in the world. Did you ever stop to think about the things God created which are not (it would seem) necessary for life? Does food have to taste good to be nutritious, to keep you alive? Is it possible to exist without beauty? Could mankind still exist if there were no beautiful sunsets? No magnificent mountains? No sparkling springs? No flowers? No rose bushes? Of course, it would be possible for the human race to exist without beauty—just as it is possible for hardened criminals to live out a life sentence in a drab prison. Could we live without bananas or peaches or grapes? Of course we could! Then why did God put us on a world brimming with beautiful (and delicious) things? He did not have to. He could have created some kind of plant to grow something that would be the equivalent of World War II K rations—nutritious but not delicious. He could have made a dull, drab world, but He did not. He made a beautiful world!

Why? Perhaps because He wanted to give human beings something to enjoy. After all, He made man with the ability to "find enjoyment," thus to find happiness during his time on earth. If He made people capable of enjoying life, and He created a world full of things they could enjoy, we conclude that God's plan was for us to enjoy our life on this planet.

That life should, ideally, be enjoyable is a truth celebrated throughout the ages. There are sayings like "Laugh, and the world laughs with you," and songs which say things like, "Put on a happy face."

How can one find happiness or enjoyment in this life, even if "all is vanity"? Solomon has a lot to say on that subject, and we will consider his advice in the next three lessons. But first we want to notice that the New Testament advises followers of Christ to enjoy life.

Should Christians Enjoy Life? Answer Yes!

The gospel overflows with joy. When Jesus was born, an angel told the shepherds, "I bring you good news of great joy which will be for all the people" (Luke 2:10). When He gave the beatitudes, Jesus said that if one did what he told His followers to do he or she would be "blessed" or happy (Matt 5:1–12). The apostle Paul wrote, "Rejoice in the Lord always; again I will say, rejoice!" (Phil 4:4) and "rejoice always" (1 Thess 5:16).

Christians, therefore, should not go around with long faces, always frowning, constantly disapproving, consistently serious and sober, never smiling or laughing or joking. They have good reasons to be happy; indeed, they should be, as a rule, the happiest people on earth.[2]

And if God's children are happy, and if they show that they are happy, they may find it easier to convert others to Christ. People who are lost are more likely to be attracted to a religion if its members show that they enjoy life. The fact is: Everyone likes to be around a person who enjoys life more than he or she wants to be around someone who is always unhappy.

In other words, the wise man's advice to his hearers to "enjoy life" is good advice for us today.

Conclusion

However, one more thing needs to be said. The advice of Ecclesiastes (like that of the book of Proverbs) is good advice for all, regardless of whether they are among God's people or not. If you were an unbeliever, it would still be better for you if you lived in such a way as to find enjoyment.

But when the New Testament speaks of happiness, it usually refers to the joy that comes from obeying God and having one's sins forgiven. For example, after the Ethiopian treasurer became a Christian—after he had his sins washed away by the blood of Christ when he was baptized—he "went on his way rejoicing" (Acts 8:39). Similarly, after the day of Pentecost, when three thousand obeyed the command to "repent and be baptized," those who had become Christians ate together "with gladness and sincerity of heart" (Acts 2:46). When you have been forgiven by God, when you are His child, you have reason to rejoice even when bad things happen to you. The apostles were beaten for failing to obey the Jewish rulers' command not to preach in the name of Jesus, but they left the place of their flogging "rejoicing that they had been considered worthy to suffer shame for His name" (Acts 5:41; they were doing what Jesus told them to do in Matt 5:10, 11).

So if you want to be able to "rejoice evermore," the best advice you could get would be: Begin to follow Jesus by becoming a Christian and having your sins forgiven!

Discussion Questions

1. Solomon in the book of Ecclesiastes says over and over again that life is vain, or meaningless. Yet much of the book contains positive teachings which will help one live

more successfully. How can these two aspects of the book of Ecclesiastes be reconciled? What do you think of the idea that Solomon is saying something like, "Life is meaningless, but we have to live it, so let's make the best of a bad situation by living wisely and successfully"? Do you have a better way of interpreting the positive instructions found in Ecclesiastes?

2. Discuss the idea that Christians should enjoy life. Could this premise be taken to an unbiblical extreme (would it be right to say that a Christian sins if he does not enjoy life?)? What is there about Christianity that, in your opinion, makes life enjoyable?

3. Discuss: Can we conclude from Solomon's teachings (as well as from other teachings in the Bible) that a person's happiness depends not so much on his external circumstances as on his internal attitudes?

4. Think about suicide. Suicide has been (and may continue to be) regarded as a very honorable way to end one's life in some cultures. It also seems very common today. Why do you think so many people (and so many young people) kill themselves? Is there anything Christian about such a response? Is

there anything to be done—or anything we can do—to help solve this modern problem?

Endnotes

1. Abimelech, Samson, Saul, Saul's amour-bearer, Ahithophel, Zimri in the Old Testament, Judas in the New Testament.

2. There are, of course, occasions when Christians should weep instead of expressing joy. Paul, for example, said, "Rejoice with those who rejoice, and weep with those who weep" (Rom 12:15). The idea is that as a rule Christians will be happy people, rejoicing constantly.

10. How To Lead an Enjoyable Life: Seventeen Suggestions (1)

According to Ecclesiastes, we need to make the best of our life in a meaningless universe. How do we do that? By enjoying life! But how can we enjoy life? By living the way we ought to live. And the way we ought to live is summed up in one word: wisdom! Live wisely and you will live the good life—a life full of enjoyment!

Solomon over and over says that we should be wise and not foolish.

- Wisdom with an inheritance is good and an advantage to those who see the sun. For wisdom is protection just as money is protection, but the advantage of knowledge is that wisdom preserves the lives of its possessors. (7:11, 12)

- Wisdom strengthens a wise man more than ten rulers who are in a city. (7:19)
- Who is like the wise man and who knows the interpretation of a matter? A man's wisdom illumines him and causes his stern face to beam. (8:1)
- Wisdom is better than strength . . . The words of the wise heard in quietness are better than the shouting of a ruler among fools. Wisdom is better than weapons of war . . . (9:16–18)
- A little foolishness is weightier than wisdom and honor. A wise man's heart directs him toward the right, but the foolish man's heart directs him toward the left. Even when the fool walks along the road, his sense is lacking and he demonstrates to everyone that he is a fool. (10:1–3)

Thus, Solomon says that if we live wisely, we will experience a good life. We will enjoy life, in spite of the fact that life on this earth is "vain" and "striving after wind." But what does it mean to be wise? Let us consider the answers that Ecclesiastes gives to that question by looking at seventeen suggestions found in the book of Ecclesiastes.

(We call them "suggestions" and not "laws" because that is what they are in the book of Ecclesiastes: suggestions about how you can live a good life. For example, one of those "suggestions" is "be willing to take a risk." That is good advice, but it is not a divine imperative—equivalent in the Old Testament to "thou shalt not kill" or in the New Testament to the command to believe in Jesus—; one would not be condemned and lost if he was too cautious and was unable to take risks. Of course, if one of these "suggestions" is found elsewhere in scripture where it is presented as "law," then it is to be regarded as "law," as well as good advice.)

ONE: FEAR GOD. To put first things first, if we would live wisely and so enjoy life, we need to fear God. In his final words to his readers, the author of Ecclesiastes says that "the whole duty of man" (KJV) is to "fear God and keep His commandments." But that is not the first time in the book that he has told his readers to fear God. In five other verses—3:14; 5:7; 7:18; 8:12, 13—we read that we should "fear God."

What does it mean to "fear God"? In Ecclesiastes 12:13 the expression summarizes what should be our attitude toward God. We should fear Him, respect Him, stand in awe of Him, to the extent that we always seek to obey Him. And we should fear Him because of eternal consequences—because God will bring everything we do into judgment. Fearing God, it is implied in those last verses of the book, will result in your going to heaven.

But the fear of God will also help you live successfully. Therefore, if you want to be happy, if you want to enjoy life, if you want to live the best kind of life possible here "under the sun," fear God and live righteously.

What would that include?

For one thing, according to Ecclesiastes, it would include taking a stand publicly in favor of God and His way. Notice 8:12, 13:

> Although a sinner does evil a hundred times and may lengthen his life, still I know it will be well for those who fear God, who fear Him openly. But it will not be well for the evil man and he will not lengthen his days like a shadow, because he does not fear God.

Those who "fear Him openly" will do well in this life. In some sense, they will be better off than those who are, in every respect, sinners, who do not fear God. A child of God should not brag about his righteousness, but neither should he try to conceal his beliefs or hide his religion.

In addition, one who fears God will offer sacrifices to Him and will pay his vows to God. Listen to the following:

> Guard your steps as you go to the house of God and draw near to listen rather than to offer the sacrifice of fools; for they do not know they are doing evil. Do not

be hasty in word or impulsive in thought to bring up a matter in the presence of God. For God is in heaven and you are on the earth; therefore let your words be few. For the dream comes through much effort and the voice of a fool through many words. When you make a vow to God, do not be late in paying it; for He takes no delight in fools. Pay what you vow! It is better that you should not vow than that you should vow and not pay. Do not let your speech cause you to sin and do not say in the presence of the messenger of God that it was a mistake. Why should God be angry on account of your voice and destroy the work of your hands? For in many dreams and in many words there is emptiness. Rather, fear God (5:1–7).

This passage mentions several things regarding our responsibilities to God.

1. When we offer sacrifices to God—in our case, when we worship God—we should listen to Him rather than just talking to Him. This suggests we need a compliant, receptive, reverent attitude in worship.
2. The idea that we should not be "hasty" or "impulsive" in worship may suggest that we need to be thoughtful and careful to follow God's directions when we worship Him—

rather than just doing the first thing that
comes to mind.

3. The fact that "God is in heaven and you are
   on the earth" suggests that God knows more
   about how He wants us to worship and serve
   Him than we know.

4. As the Israelites were told to pay their vows,
   we should remember to "pay what we vow"
   to God. For instance, we are to give as we
   have purposed (2 Cor 9:7); so let us pay what
   we have purposed. And when we became
   Christians, we, in effect, promised the rest of
   our lives to Christ. Let us make good on that
   pledge.

However, the main thing we need to remember
when we think about "fearing God" in this context is
that if we do, life will be more meaningful, we will be
happier, and we will probably be more successful.
God's rules were given, at least in part, to help us live
the good life, the abundant life, the happy life.

Thus the command to "fear God" is included with
instructions about how to live because Solomon knew
that to live successfully in this life (as well as to go to
heaven), to live wisely, to enjoy life, you should do what
is necessary to please God.

The Old Law promised blessings in this life to Israel
if they obeyed God. In our age, Jesus said that those

who follow him would enjoy abundant living (John 10:10), and He said, "Everyone who has left houses or brothers or sisters or father or mother or children or farms for my name's sake will receive many times as much, and will inherit eternal life" (Matt 19:29). Our reward for serving God is not just "pie in the sky by and by." Rather, we will live the best life possible if we seek to do God's will in everything while we live on this earth.

TWO: DO THINGS IN A TIMELY MANNER. One of the more interesting passages in Ecclesiastes is 3:1–8:

There is an appointed time for everything.

And there is a time for every event under heaven—

A time to give birth and a time to die;

A time to plant and a time to uproot what is planted;

A time to kill and a time to heal;

A time to tear down and a time to build up;

A time to weep and a time to laugh;

A time to mourn and a time to dance;

A time to throw stones and a time to gather stones;

A time to embrace and a time to shun embracing;

A time to search and a time to give up as lost;

A time to keep and a time to throw away;

A time to tear apart and a time to sew together;

A time to be silent and a time to speak;

A time to love and a time to hate;

A time for war and a time for peace.

Probably the point of this passage is that the natural cycles of life are so repetitious, so boring, so constant and predictable, that life itself is tedious and tiring and vain. Why bother to try to make a difference by building, for instance, when there will come a time when the building will be torn down? The next verse seems to confirm that something like this was on Solomon's mind. He says in verse 9: "What profit is there to the worker from that in which he toils?"

However, Solomon may also have intended to remind his readers that they needed to exercise common sense in their use of time. Solomon hints at the same idea when he says in chapter 8, "The wise heart knows *the proper time* and procedure" (8:5). Maybe in these passages he was saying, "Be wise in your use of time. Choose carefully not only what you do but also when you do it." For instance, have we all not got into trouble from talking when we should have been listening? Is it not smarter to approach your boss for a raise when you have done something right rather than just after he has reprimanded you? Are there not times—when everyone around you is crying—when it would be better not to tell your best joke? If someone is worried about where his next meal is coming from, maybe that is not the best time to try to teach him the gospel. Maybe you should feed him first, teach him second. The New Testament says something similar when it tells Christians: "Be careful how you walk, not as unwise but as wise, making the most of your time, because the days are evil" (Eph 5:16).

THREE: WORK, DO NOT SHIRK. Solomon writes in Ecclesiastes 4:5, "The fool folds his hands and consumes his own flesh." He makes the same point again by saying that "Through indolence the rafters sag, and through slackness the house leaks" (10:18). From a positive standpoint, Solomon recommends that human beings work hard for a living (though their efforts in the end may be in vain; see the lesson on "What About Work?").

The New Testament also teaches us to work (see Eph 4:28; 2 Thess 3:10). And we can see the wisdom in it. If you want to succeed—and to be happy in life—if you want to live wisely and so to enjoy life—you need to work, and work hard, at your occupation.

FOUR: DO NOT FORGET TO REST. Even though the writer of Ecclesiastes urges his readers to work, he also implies that they should take time to rest. In 4:6 we read: "One handful of rest is better than two fists full of labor and striving after wind." The fact that God made the rest required by the Sabbath law part of the Ten Command-ments proves that God recognized man's need for "R & R"—rest and recreation. We do not live under the Law of Moses, therefore we do not live under the Sabbath law. But we still need to recognize our need to rest.

FIVE: MAKE FRIENDS. Sometimes talented people are denied the success you would expect them to experience because they have never learned to work with others. They may have few friends, or no friends. "I'll do it myself" has always been their motto. "I don't need anyone's help."

In contrast to that attitude, the book of Ecclesiastes indicates the value of having friends, companions, advisers, on whom you can depend in your daily life. Listen to the wise man:

> Two are better than one because they have a good return for their labor. For if either of them falls, the one will lift up his companion. But woe to the one who falls when there is not another to lift him up. Furthermore if two lie down together they keep warm, but how can one be warm alone? And if one can overpower him who is alone, two can resist him. A cord of three strands is not quickly torn apart (4:9–12).

Solomon says if you have a friend, he can help you with your work, pick you up when you fall, help you keep warm when you are cold, and help defend you when you are attacked! The value of having such a friend ought to be obvious. A friend can advise us, comfort us, help us, encourage us, strengthen us. Whatever we do, it is better to do it with a friend. We are more likely to succeed if have the help of a friend.

Because of the value of friendship—of having others who can and will encourage and help you—God gave us the church and our brothers and sisters in the church, along with instructions like these: "Bear one another's burdens" (Gal 6:2); encourage "one another" (Heb 10:25); "comfort one another" (1 Thess 4:18); "confess your sins to one another and pray for one another" (Jas 5:16). The church is a "one another" body, and we need to enjoy being part of the lives of others and their being a part of our lives.

Similarly, out in the world, if we want to enjoy life, we need to reject the practice of "rugged individualism" and make friends who can help us throughout our lives. Probably people with a talent for making friends are more likely to do well in life than people who are talented but have to work alone. Remember what the wise man said: "Two are better than one."

SIX: DO NOT TALK TOO MUCH. Several times Solomon seems to equate foolishness with talking too much. In 6:11 he says, "For there are many words which increase futility." In 5:2 he says, "Let your words be few," and in the next verse he associates "many words" with "the voice of a fool." Later in chapter 5, he says, "In many words there is emptiness" (5:7b). Then in 10:12–14a we read:

> Words from the mouth of a wise man are gracious, while the lips of a fool consume him; the beginning of his talking is folly and the end of it is wicked madness. Yet the fool multiplies words.

In this last passage, according to Solomon, the wise man speaks "gracious words"—words which build up and encourage and help others. The fool, in contrast, speaks "folly," especially in that he "multiplies words"— he talks too much!

We probably agree with Solomon that it is foolish to talk too much, and that talking too much at the wrong time can keep one from success and happiness. The New Testament also agrees: James wrote, "Everyone must be quick to hear, *slow to speak* and slow to anger" (Jas 1:19). The problem many of us have is that we listen too little and talk too much. If we want to enjoy life, we need to reverse that tendency.

SEVEN: STRIVE TO HAVE A GOOD NAME. Solomon says, "A good name is better than a good ointment" (7:1a). We all ought to be able to see the truth of that fact. Your "name"—your reputation, what people think of you—is tremendously important in determining how you get along in life, in whether you succeed or not.

How do you acquire a "good name"? You will not acquire it by being totally unconcerned about what people think of you. Granted, we need to be more concerned about what God thinks—about doing what is right—than we are about what other human beings think. But that does not mean we should care nothing about what our neighbors see in us or think about us. Paul indicated that he was concerned about what others thought when he wrote, "I have become all things to all men, so that I may by all means save some" (1 Cor 9:22; see the context). We, too, should be concerned about what others think of us, about having a "good name"—if for no other reason than to have a better chance at influencing them for good.

How can we acquire a good name? The best way is to put on the Christian characteristics spoken of in the New Testament. For instance, Ephesians 4 tells us to put aside falsehood and speak the truth, to take care not to let our anger cause us to sin but instead to forgive the wrongs which are done to us, to abstain from stealing but to work for a living instead, to speak only words which edify (build up), to rid ourselves of bitterness and wrath and anger and clamor and slander and malice but to be kind and tender-hearted and forgiving. (Eph 4:22–32) If we will act like that, chances are we will have a "good name" in our society.

Discussion Questions

1. The seventeen suggestions found in this lesson and the two that follow were chosen more or less arbitrarily by the author of this series. As you read through the book, can you see other ideas that might be included in such a list? If so, please share them with the class and discuss them.

2. "Fear God" is found in the conclusion of the book and several times earlier. Does that admonition sound strange? Is it possible to "fear God" and to "love God" at the same time? What do you think it mans to "fear God"? If you have access to a commentary or commentaries, what do others say it means?

3. Discuss the suggestion "work, do not shirk." Do you think this is an admonition that is needed today? Are there people who expect to be paid even though they are unwilling to work?

4. Do you agree with the following: Just as there are some who do not understand the need to work, there are others who do not understand the need to rest. Have you ever known anyone like that? What are the consequences for the individual and his

family if he never takes any time off for
"R & R"?

5. "Make friends" is one suggestion. Note what
   Solomon says about why two are better than
   one. Do you agree? Do some people make
   friends more easily than others? How can we
   —even if it doesn't come naturally—make
   friends who will help us meet the challenges
   of life? Are there dangers involved in having
   friends? (Hint: Can friends lead you astray?)

6. How important is it to "have a good name"?
   How do you achieve that end? If you have
   "messed up" in the past, so that you now have
   a bad reputation, what can or should you do
   to restore, or cultivate for the first time, a
   good name?

11. How to Lead an Enjoyable Life: Seventeen Suggestion (2)

E IGHT: *CONTROL YOUR ANGER.* Ecclesiastes warns against anger. We read, "Do not be eager in your heart to be angry, for anger resides in the bosom of fools" (7:9). In other words, wise men do not get angry often, but fools do. Most of us would agree: We have seen "fools" get angry and lash out in ways that hurt only them. We can surely see that it would be harder for a quick-tempered person to succeed and find happiness in life than it would be for one who does a good job of controlling whatever anger he feels.

At the same time, in this case, as in others, we need to make sure we do not misunderstand what is being taught. Ecclesiastes does not make a rule: "Thou shalt never get angry." Biblically speaking, there is a time and place for what we would call "righteous anger"—when, for instance, we see evil triumph or the poor or disabled taken advantage of. Even if we do become "righteously" angry when we see such things, we must not do what the Bible forbids. We must not, for instance, personally hurt or kill the people who are doing wrong. It is possible to become angry without sinning (Eph 4:26).

However, even if we admit that there are times when there is nothing wrong with becoming angry, we should also agree that the anger most people experience most of the time is not righteous anger. Someone cuts me off in traffic, and I respond by getting angry—that is not righteous anger. If I am playing basketball and someone fouls me intentionally, and I react by getting angry and hitting back—that is not righteous anger. If someone says something particularly nasty about me, and I react with angry words—that is not righteous anger.

We need to avoid getting angry about such things. As James said, we need to be "slow to anger" (Jas 1:19).

NINE: DO NOT LIVE IN THE PAST. Or, as Ecclesiastes puts it: "Do not say, 'Why is it that the former days were better than these?' For it is not from wisdom that you ask about this" (7:10). For those of us who are older, this advice hits close to home. Have you ever known an old person (including this writer) who did not spend a lot of his or her time comparing the present age with the "olden days"? And, of course, the "olden days" were aways better. Solomon's advice to us is: Forget it! It is foolish to waste time thinking about whether the past was better or worse; we cannot change it (though we might be able to learn from it). The important thing is the here and now—and the future. That is what the wise person is concerned about. Paul put it well: "Forgetting what lies behind and reaching forward to what lies ahead, I press on toward the goal for the prize of the upward call of God in Christ Jesus" (Phil 3:13, 14).

TEN: EXPECT GOD TO SEND BOTH PROSPERITY AND ADVERSITY. Solomon says, "In the day of prosperity be happy, but in the day of adversity consider— God has made the one as well as the other" (7:14). This verse gives us several things to think about:

We should be happy in days of prosperity. For most of us, that includes most days. Happiness should be the customary characteristic of our personal existence. The New Testament says, "Rejoice always" (1 Thess 5:16).

There will come days of adversity. We do not live in a "health and wealth" universe in which the Christian is always protected from trouble. Solomon writes:

> It is better to go to a house of mourning than to go to a house of feasting, because that is the end of every man, and the living takes it to heart. Sorrow is better than laughter ... (7:2, 3a).

Solomon's main point is that life is vain because it

is full of sorrow and characterized by death. However, one who realizes that life is not always easy, that life is hard, that people all experience disappointments, that death is an ever-present reality, is wiser than one who tries to skip through life, thinking all is always well, and that one can expect nothing but good times and good things throughout his or her life.

In other words, the wise person realizes that bad things are likely to happen—adversity will come—, and therefore when negative things do occur, that person is not as upset as he would have been otherwise. He or she is able to experience what men call "bad luck" and deal with it.

Both prosperity and adversity come from God. That is a message we may not like to hear. We are happy to credit God with giving us good things, but we have to find someone else to blame when bad things happen. When we do that, we may have the best of intentions, but we are ignoring one thing: the sovereignty of God. God is in charge of this universe. Nothing happens unless He causes it to happen or allows it to happen. So if it happens, we can truthfully say, "God did it" or "God permitted it." (God of course does not cause men to sin or tempt men to sin; nevertheless, He allows Satan to have the opportunity to tempt men, and He allows men the opportunity to sin, to give in to Satan's temptations.) Remember: after Satan tempted Job by taking away what he had, Job said, with God's approval, *"The Lord gave and the Lord has taken away*. Blessed be the name of the Lord" (Job 1:21b).

Is there value in recognizing that adversity, as well as prosperity, comes from God? It should be comforting to know that God is in charge of the universe. We can therefore believe that whatever happens is part of a bigger picture; God is doing something and He knows what He is doing, even if we do not; and whatever happens to us is part of God's great plan. In addition, God has given us assurance that He will not allow us to be tempted above what we are able (1 Cor 10:13) and that "all things [that happen in a Christian's life] work together for good" (Rom 8:28, KJV).

In the sense that the wise man knows that he will have negative experiences and so he prepares to deal with them, that wise person is more likely to succeed in life than the overly optimistic individual who lives with the notion that nothing bad can ever happen to him.

ELEVEN: AVOID EXTREMES, LEAD A WELL-BALANCED LIFE. In Ecclesiastes 7:16–18 we find these interesting words from Solomon's pen:

> Do not be excessively righteous and do not be overly wise. Why should you ruin yourself? Do not be excessively wicked and do not be a fool. Why should you die before your time? It is good that you grasp one

thing and also not let go of the other; for the one who fears God comes forth with both of them (7:16–18).

It would be hard to be "excessively righteous" or "overly wise." Solomon must be saying something like "Do not make a show of your righteousness or your wisdom. And do not be so concerned about righteousness and wisdom that you forget everything else— that is, do not emphasize righteousness or foolishness so much that you are no longer of any practical use to anyone." We say something similar when we say of someone that he is "so heavenly minded as to be of no earthly use." Then when Solomon says, in effect, "Do not choose; take both of them," he may be saying something like, "Lead a well-balanced life. You do not have to choose, for example, between being a good student and a good athlete; be both!"

Today, Christians should not make a show of their religion, as did the Pharisees in Jesus's day, and they should realize that their religion involves, not just going to church, but everything they do! No one will accuse the faithful Christian of being "excessively righteous" because he goes to church and, in addition, visits the fatherless and widows, is a hard worker, and is kind to everyone.

Furthermore, he will be wise if he avoids going to extremes in other matters. Recreation is good, but we do not need sixteen hours of recreation every day.

Reading is good, but no one needs to read all day every day. One can be a sports fan but needs to be careful not to be too fanatical. A Christian might even become so engrossed in his religion that he cannot talk about anything but religion. If he does, people will probably look at him as if he is crazy and quietly move away. He will have no chance to win them to Christ.

So … if you want to be successful and happy, avoid extremes and lead a well-balanced life. "Let your moderation be known unto all men" (Phil 4:5, KJV).

TWELVE: DO NOT WORRY ABOUT THE NEGA- TIVE THINGS PEOPLE SAY ABOUT YOU. The book of Ecclesiastes says that you should not be concerned about everything you hear. We read, "Do not take seri- ously all words which are spoken, so that you will not hear your servant cursing you" (7:21). The idea seems to be that one should not get too upset when his servant curses him—maybe because that is what he should expect to hear. We can apply it to ourselves by resolving not to worry about all the negative things we hear about ourselves.

The fact is that anyone who tries to do anything worthwhile will be criticized. And anyone who tries to live right will make enemies. And anyone who has enemies will find that those enemies will likely say bad things about him—maybe even tell lies about him. If you are the object of such verbal attacks, how should you react? Solomon gives good advice when he says we should "not take seriously" the attacks made on our character. Sometimes it is best simply to overlook such criticism; to say, "Sticks and stones may break my bones, but words will never hurt me." Obviously, It would never be right to respond in kind—if we are cursed, to respond by cursing. In that kind of situation, we would need to follow Jesus' example: He was "reviled," but He did not "revile in return" (1 Pet 2:23).

Of course, there are times when we need to hear the criticism of friends and foes alike, and then change our ways. Still, if we want to succeed and be happy in life we cannot take seriously every negative word we hear from others about ourselves.

THIRTEEN: STRIVE TO HAVE A GOOD MARRIAGE. Most of us would agree that if we are happy at home—if our marriage and family life is enjoyable—we are happy, period. Nothing affects our overall sense of wellbeing as much as our family life does. How can you have a have a good marriage? Ecclesiastes gives two suggestions.

One: Marry the right person, and stay married to him or her. And, of course, the "right person" means a person you can and will love throughout your life. Ecclesiastes includes these memorable words:

> Enjoy life with the woman whom you love all the days of your fleeting life which He has given to you under the sun; for this is your reward in life … (9:9a).

Other versions have: "Live joyfully with the wife whom thou lovest all the days of the life of thy vanity" (KJV); "enjoy life with the wife whom you love" (NRSV, NIV); "life is short, and you love your wife, so enjoy being with her" (CEV).

The idea is clear: A man and a woman fall in love and get married. Then they can enjoy themselves for the rest of their lives.

Let that be your story. There are too many people who get married and then divorce. There are too many people who do not marry at all but live with partners to whom they are not married. There are too many men who father children but never take responsibility for them. There are too many "single-parent" families. And there are those who think that the bonding of homosexuals is marriage. A breakdown in marriage means a breakdown of the family and is likely to lead to a breakdown of the nation! Stay married! That was Jesus's plan. When He was asked about divorce, he replied,

Have you not read that He who created them from the beginning made them male and female, and said, "For this reason a man shall leave his father and mother and be joined to his wife, and the two shall become one flesh"? So they are no longer two, but one flesh. What therefore God has joined together, let no man separate (Matt 19:4–6).

Jesus believed in and taught: One man, one wife, for life!

It can be done: my parents had their 68th anniversary before my mother died; my wife's parents were married more than 50 years before her father died; my brother and his wife were married 64 years before she died; my wife's brother and his wife have been married more than 50 years; my wife and I celebrated our 62nd anniversary before she died; our two daughters have been married 41 and 34 years.

The point is: If some people can stay married for fifty or sixty years, so can you! What will it take? Love that woman you married (or, if you are a woman, that man you married) from the time you married her "as long as you both shall live."

A second requirement for a happy marriage is suggested by the following words from Ecclesiastes 7:26:

> And I discovered more bitter than death the woman whose heart is snares and nets, whose hands are chains. One who is pleasing to God will escape from her, but the sinner will be captured by her.

To stay married—to have a successful marriage and good family—stay away from those of the opposite sex who could tempt you to commit adultery. Solomon, both here and in the book of Proverbs, warns against evil women—perhaps prostitutes—who can lead men astray. But the act of adultery does not necessarily start with a prostitute or a "loose woman." It can be instigated by a lustful male or a lonely co-worker or come as the result of a long friendship. The point is that if you want to have a happy marriage, you have to stay faithful to your spouse!

In today's word, that sounds like a revolutionary idea. The modern view is: "As long as someone does not get hurt, sex outside of marriage, or with someone other than your spouse, is okay." That is not the biblical view! Sex outside of marriage is adultery! And adultery was regarded as sufficiently serious under the Old Testament Law to be punishable by death! Adultery was a sin then, and it is a sin today.

Think about it this way: God made human beings, and He instituted marriage. He knows what is best for mankind. And what is best for us is that we marry one we love and stay married to her or him and remain faithful to her or him the rest of our lives! If we do, we will experience a more successful, more enjoyable life, than we would if we had done something different.

Discussion Questions

1. How does the advice not to worry about the negative things people say about you relate to the present-day determination not to be

"dissed"—disrespected. Many people are likely to fight, some even to kill, if they are "dissd." Does Solomon's advice go contrary to this tendency? If so, should you follow Solomon's advice? Why do people resent being "dissed"? What's the Christian solution for this problem?

2. How hard is it for you to "control your anger"? Do some people have more trouble than others doing so? What are the consequences which are likely to occur if one does not control his or her anger? Can you give examples of the negative effects of uncontrolled anger? What can one do to help him/her keep his/her anger under control?

3. "Do not live in the past." Do older people have a greater tendency to "live in the past" than young people? Why? What should a young person do when an older person seems to constantly want to talk about the past? How can an older person keep from living in the past?

4. Do you think you live what could be called a "well-balanced life"? What could you do to make that expression describe your life?

5. Discuss: The importance of a good marriage, especially its relationship to leading a happy, successful life. Do you think this idea is

accepted by the majority of the population in America today? (Especially if you judge what is happening in this country by what you see on TV and in the movies.) Some suggestions are given in the lesson about how to have a successful marriage. Can you think of others? Think of couples who have long, happy, successful marriages. How did, or how do, they do it?

6. Discuss one or all of the following in the light of the teachings of the Bible: Same-sex marriage. Living together without being married. Single women having to raise children on their own. The prevalence of divorce.

7. Do you think one is more likely to be successful if he/she expects to experience both prosperity and adversity in life? If one expects nothing but prosperity, what might happen to him/her if misfortune occurs?

8. Discuss: Is it biblical to say that God sends adversity as well as prosperity? Can you cite scripture for your position?

12. How to Lead an Enjoyable Life: Seventeen Suggestions (3)

FOURTEEN: RESPECT AUTHORITY. Solomon wrote,

> I say, "Keep the command of the king because of the oath before God. Do not be in a hurry to leave him. Do not join in an evil matter, for he will do whatever he pleases. Since the word of the king is authoritative, who will say to him, 'What are you doing?' He who keeps a royal command experiences no trouble, for a wise heart knows the proper time and procedure" (8:2–5).

In addition, he wrote, "If the ruler's temper rises against you, do not abandon your position, because composure allays great offenses" (10:4). He also said, "Furthermore, in your bedchamber do not curse a king, and in your sleeping rooms do not curse a rich man, for a bird of the heavens will carry the sound and the winged creature will make the matter known" (10:20).

Solomon's advice regarding the king is very practical:

1. Keep the king's commands because you have sworn a vow (perhaps all Israelites were obligated to vow allegiance to the king).
2. Do not join in a conspiracy against the king.
3. Do not expect the king to do what you say. He is in charge and will do what he wants to do.
4. Keep your composure if you are confronted by the king about something you have said. Do not deny saying it. Just face the king as an able, confident person.
5. Do not say bad things about the king or about others in authority. If you do, somehow the word will get back to them and you will be held accountable for what you said.

Solomon's advice here seems to be quite self-serving. He was the king. He was, in effect, saying, "Obey me!" However, even though it was good for the king for his subjects to obey him, it was even better for them to do so. Otherwise, they might end up punished, imprisoned, even executed. Think about it: You are the subject of a king. He makes a decree you do not like. Maybe he raises the taxes by ten per cent. What do you do? Protest? And end up in jail. Refuse to pay the extra taxes? And end up having your farm confiscated. Lead a rebellion against the king? And end up dead. It is just good advice to do what the king says. In the long run, you will be alive, out of prison, and better off.

Similarly today: There are good reasons to obey the law, and one of them is: If you break the law you are likely to get caught and be punished! Consequently: respect authority, obey the law, and you will lead a better, happier, more successful life.

Christians have an additional reason to respect authority, to obey the laws of the land. God commands it! Jesus clearly said we should pay our taxes to Caesar —to the secular ruler (Matt 22:21). Paul wrote, "Every person is to be subject to the governing authorities" (Rom 13:1; see vv. 1–7). Peter wrote, "Submit yourselves for the Lord's sake to every human institution, whether to a king as one in authority, or to governors as sent by him for the punishment of evildoers and the praise of those who do right ... honor the king" (1 Pet 2:13, 14, 17d).

If the law of the land would prevent us from doing the will of God, then we would have to obey God rather than man (Acts 5:29); otherwise Christians are commanded to obey secular authorities.

The main point, however, is that to respect authority, to respect those who make the laws and enforce the laws, and to obey the law, is better for *you!* You will be happier, you will live a more enjoyable life, you will be more successful if you respect authority.

FIFTEEN: DO THINGS ENTHUSIASTICALLY. The author of Ecclesiastes makes the point that if one hopes to succeed, he needs to give himself wholeheartedly to the task he is working on. Listen to these words:

> Whatever your hand finds to do, do it with all your might; for there is no activity or planning or knowledge or wisdom in Sheol where you are going (9:10).

The importance of this advice should be obvious. My mother taught me that "if a thing's worth doing, it is worth doing right." Consequently, all my life if I did something I tried to do the best I could under the circumstances. If people approved—if they applauded or admired my efforts—I was grateful. But to me more important was the question: Had I done my best? If I had, I was satisfied, no matter what others thought.

If you follow Solomon's advice: If you are a preacher, you will be the best preacher possible. If you are a farmer, you will be the best farmer you can be. If you are a sales clerk, you will be the best sales clerk possible. If you play football or basketball or volleyball, you will be the best player you can be, if you are a student you will be the best student you can be. Whatever you do, you will do it wholeheartedly. And if you work wholeheartedly at everything you do, chances are you will be successful.

The New Testament suggests that we should work hard at whatever we do. Slaves were told to obey their masters, not just with "external service," but "with sincerity of heart, fearing the Lord" (Col 3:23). Christians were told that they should always *abound* in the work of the Lord (1 Cor 15:58). So whether you work for a human boss or serve the Lord above, you should do so with all your heart! If you do, you will be far more likely to experience success in life.

SIXTEEN: PREPARE FOR WHAT YOU ARE GOING TO DO. In 10:10 we read, "If the axe is dull and he does not sharpen its edge, then he must exert more strength. Wisdom has the advantage of giving success." It is easy to understand what Solomon is saying here. If you are going to chop wood with an axe, you need to sharpen it first. If you do not, but leave it dull, then you may still be able to cut the wood, but it will take considerably more effort. Solomon attributes this willingness to "sharpen your axe" before you begin to work to "wisdom." Wisdom—sharpening your axe before your work —has the advantage of giving success.

Likewise today: You save time and effort and money if you prepare for whatever it is you are planning to do. Some of the time I follow that rule, but not always. When I drove to a distant destination with which I was unfamiliar, I thought it was unmanly and sissy-like, to look at the map ahead of time to try to find out how to get there—much less to write down what turns to take when. The result was often a meandering journey in which we saw a lot of territory but got to our destination hours later than we had planned. My wife, in contrast, liked to look it up on a map, then write it down—how to go, when to turn, how far, etc. Like I say, she was a sissy! But she got us there on time! My point? By refusing to prepare ahead of time, I made a less successful journey than I would have if I had "sharpened my axe"—if I had made proper preparation.

Today, if you want to be successful, you need to "sharpen your axe." You may be able to accomplish something without doing any preparation, but it will be harder, and chances are you will not accomplish as much. Thus, as you think about your future, "sharpen your axe" by preparing yourself. For some, that would mean getting a college education; for others, learning a trade; for all of us, it would probably mean thinking about what we are going to do, and making plans and preparing ourselves, before we start a task.

It is simply good advice: If you want to succeed in life, "sharpen your axe"—prepare ahead of time for what you plan to do.

SEVENTEEN: BE WILLING TO TAKE A RISK. In

one of the more memorable passages in Ecclesiastes, the author writes:

> Cast your bread on the surface of the waters, for you will find it after many days. Divide your portion to seven or even to eight, for you do not know what misfortune may occur on the earth ... .He who watches the wind will not sow and he who looks at the clouds will not reap. Just as you do not know the path of the wind, and how bones are formed in the womb of the pregnant woman, so you do not know the activity of God who makes all things. Sow your seed in the morning ... (11:1, 2, 4, 5, 6a).

"Cast your bread on the waters." In other words, be willing to take a risk, to try to achieve something even if there is no guarantee that you will succeed ... maybe even if it is unlikely that you will achieve it.

Of course, there is value in looking ahead, weighing pros and cons, thinking carefully before undertaking a task. When one begins a new project, he asks himself such questions as: "Can I do this—do I have the resources I need—the skills it takes—to get this done in a timely manner? And even if I can get it done, will it do anyone any good? Or will I have wasted my time?"

However, after asking all those questions, one should still be willing to risk his efforts even if there is no guarantee of success. If one becomes too concerned about the possible failure of his efforts, he will never do anything. As Solomon says, "one who watches the wind will not sow and he who looks at the clouds will not reap." If you are frozen by fear of failure, you will never achieve anything. We never know what will be the outcome of our efforts, so we should go ahead and take a risk—try to succeed, try to win, try to build, even if we are not guaranteed success. As Solomon says, "sow your seed in the morning!" Take that risk! Try!

The New Testament also encourages us to sow seed, even when we know that it will not all bear fruit. In the parable of the sower, seed fell onto four kinds of soil and only one bore fruit. Should the sower have said, "My work is mostly worthless; three out of four times I fail; I'm just going to quit"? No! The sower continued to sow, even though he knew he was not guaranteed success.

In fact, the "sowers" of the gospel in New Testament times, the evangelists, went out preaching the gospel knowing, not only that not everyone would respond to their appeal, but that they were putting themselves at risk by doing so. Many were persecuted and many died because of their faithfulness in proclaiming the word of God. Every time they went out to preach to unbelievers, they risked their lives in the hope that some would be saved!

We need to be willing to do the same. Sometimes we need to have the attitude of Esther, the Jewish girl who became a Persian queen, who was asked to intercede with the king on behalf of her people who were about to be annihilated. However, if she approached the king on his throne without being invited, the law was that she would be killed unless the king held out his golden scepter to her. Knowing she was likely to die, she accepted the challenge, saying, "If I perish, I perish" (Esth 4:16). She was willing to risk her life to save her people!

Likewise, we need to keep on with our efforts to do good, to succeed, to achieve something worthwhile, and especially to spread God's word, even if the odds are against our success! We need to be willing to take a risk!

Conclusion

In conclusion, we ask again: How can one exercise wisdom with the result that he or she will live an enjoyable life "under the sun"? One would do well to follow these seventeen suggestions found in the book of Ecclesiastes:

Fear God.

Do things in a timely manner.

Work, do not shirk.

Do not forget to rest.

Do not talk too much.

Make friends.

Strive to have a good name.

Control your anger.

Do not live in the past.

Expect God to send both prosperity and adversity.

Avoid extremes, lead a well-balanced life.

Do not worry about the negative things people say about you.

Strive to have a good marriage.

Respect authority.

Do things enthusiastically.

Prepare for what you are going to do.

Be willing to take a risk.

If you want to live a good life here, a happy life, do these seventeen things. And let me emphasize that this is the smart thing—the wise thing—to do.

You may be inclined to always go it alone, to emphasize just one aspect of your life—for example, your job—to the detriment of all others, to constantly show that you dislike and disrespect authorities—such as the police—, to neglect your marriage partner. Maybe you will survive even if you do. But it is doubtful that you will really succeed, and even more doubtful that you will live a happy life!

In other words, you will be better off to follow Solomon's advice than to ignore it. It is simply the smart thing—the wise thing—to do in a world that often seems to be empty, discouraging, and meaningless. "All is vanity"—but you can still have a good life if you will let wisdom direct your steps.

Discussion Questions

1. How important is it to "respect authority"? (For example: Is a person more or less likely to go to jail if he respects authority?) Is there any biblical reason why a Christian would be justified in refusing to obey an order given by someone in authority over him/her? Must one obey only rulers who deserve his/her respect?

2. Regarding taking risks: Do you know of anyone who decided to take a risk—to try something even though there was no guarantee of success —who succeeded and profited (monetarily or otherwise) as a result? If one takes such a risk, is he (even if he is a Christian) guaranteed success? Why then take a risk? (Hint: Solomon seems to say that if we don't, we can be sure we will not experience optimum success.)

3. How important is it to prepare for what you plan to do? Can you think of examples from your experience of people who prepared for an occupation, and succeeded as a result? From a biblical standpoint, can you think of

people who spent time (sometimes without knowing it) preparing for the tasks God had for them to do? (How about the apostles? How about Saul of Tarsus?) Do you agree or disagree with the following statement: Education is not the only means of preparing for a job or for a life, but it is important for us to encourage the people we can influence to get a good education. Discuss this issue.

4. "If a thing's worth doing, it's worth doing right." Do you agree with this saying? Do you think there might be exceptions to this rule? Or that it might be overdone and lead to a kind of perfectionism that is self-defeating? Nevertheless, would we (society, the church, the family) be better off if more people had this attitude?

13. The Conclusion: Ecclesiastes 11:9–12:14

In Ecclesiastes Solomon has pronounced life to be meaningless—vanity, vain, striving after wind. That means, he says, that our pursuit of fame and fortune is really meaningless. Even if we find what we seek, it does not satisfy or it does not last long, and eventually we will be forgotten anyway. However, we can make the best of our meaningless existence by doing the things that Solomon says will allow us to enjoy life.

But following Solomon's good advice does not really give life meaning; it is still vanity and striving after wind. As we come to the end of the book we are still asking, "What is it that gives life meaning?" So far, our question remains unanswered.

Then at the very end of Ecclesiastes, the author says, "The conclusion is … ." The King James Version has "Let us hear the conclusion of the whole matter;" the

Revised Standard translates "The end of the matter; all has been heard;" and the New International Version has, "Now all has been heard; here is the conclusion of the matter."

We hear the word "conclusion" and our ears perk up. The "Conclusion" is significant. It should summarize; it should define; it should drive home the main point. It should answer the question: "If nothing we have heard about gives life meaning—or keeps it from being merely vanity—what does?"

Solomon tells us when he gets to verses 13 and 14 of chapter 12. However, before we get to that point— before we learn *the* conclusion—Solomon presents three other conclusions worth considering.

A Conclusion About Youth

First, beginning at 11:9 and continuing through 12:1a, Solomon presents his conclusion concerning youth:

> Rejoice, young man, during your childhood, and let your heart be pleasant during the days of young manhood. And follow the impulses of your heart and the desires of your eyes. Yet know that God will bring you to judgment for all these things. So, remove grief and anger from your heart and put away pain from your body, because childhood and the prime of life

are fleeting. Remember also your Creator in the days
of your youth . . . .

Solomon says that youth is a time for rejoicing, no
doubt because young people do not, as a rule, suffer the
ailments of old age that he will list in the next few
verses. Young people should, therefore, enjoy themselves by following their impulses, by doing what they
like to do. There should be no "grief" or "anger" in the
heart of a young person. At the same time, even young
people need to realize that a day of reckoning will come
when they will be called to account for what they have
done. The conclusion for youth: Enjoy yourself, but
remember you will be held accountable for what you
have done.

That is a message young people today need as well.
It is good to be young and good to enjoy what being
young means. But young people, like those who are
older, need to realize that actions have consequences.
Young people, like old people, can be involved in car
accidents, in illegal drugs, in immoral acts—and they
can suffer consequences from these things just as old
people do. More importantly: God will hold young
people, like old people, accountable for what they have
done. When young people sin, God takes note of it. The
conclusion for young people: Enjoy your youth, but
realize that God will one day call you to account.

A Conclusion About Old Age

After saying something to and about young people, Solomon turns to the other end of the age spectrum and presents what we might call his conclusions about old age:

> Remember also your Creator in the days of your youth, before the evil days come and the years draw near when you will say, "I have no delight in them"; before the sun and the light, the moon and the stars are darkened and clouds return after the rain; in the days that the watchmen of the house tremble, and mighty men stoop, the grinding ones stand idle because they are few, and those who look through windows grow dim; and the doors on the street are shut as the sound of the grinding mill is low, and one will arise at the sound of the bird, and the daughters of song will sing softly. Furthermore, men are afraid of a high place and of terrors on the road; the almond tree blossoms, the grasshopper drags himself along, and the caperberry is ineffective. For man goes to his eternal home while mourners go about the street. Remember Him before the silver cord is broken and the golden bowl is crushed, the pitcher by the well is shattered and the wheel at the cistern is crushed; then the dust will return to the earth as it was, and the spirit will return to God who gave it.

"Vanity of vanities," says the Preacher, "all is vanity!" (12:1–8)

What is getting old like? Solomon says, in the first place, old age is an "evil" time—a bad time, a hard time, an unenjoyable time, a painful time—when you will say, "I have no delight" in the days that I am living. That may be hard for some to understand or accept, but for some of us who are old, it is perfectly understandable. Old people experience pain and discomfort, suffer from a number of ailments, hardly ever go out except to see the doctor, and remember with sadness the days when they used to play golf or play softball or play basketball or maybe even shop for hours without getting tired! Those of us who are old contrast our "now" with our "then" and when Solomon speaks of the "evil days" when we shall say "I have no delight in them," all we can say is "Amen!"

Solomon then goes on to describe what it is like to get old, using a variety of figures. He describes what happens in old age as follows:[1]

- The sun, light, moon, and stars darken, and the rain returns—days of happiness grow scarce, and the clouds of unhappiness constantly recur.
- "The watchmen of the house tremble"—the arms and hands tremble.

- "Mighty men stoop"—the back is bent.
- "The grinding ones stand idle because they are few"—old people lose their teeth.
- "Those who look through the windows are dim"— the old person's eyes deteriorate; he cannot see well.
- "The sound of the grinding mill is low"— perhaps this suggests that the old person can no longer participate in communal activities like the grain harvest.
- "One rises at the sound of a bird"—the old do not sleep well, are easily awakened, and rise early.
- "The daughters of song sing softly"—perhaps they sing softly in that the old cannot hear well.
- "Men are afraid of a high place and of terrors on the road"—the old are often needlessly worried and afraid.
- "The almond tree blossoms"—the hair turns white.
- "The grasshopper drags himself along"— perhaps refers to "the laborious and ungainly walk of the elderly."
- "The caperberry is ineffective"—sexual desire fails.

Then the human being dies: He goes to his "eternal

home, while mourners go about in the street." When he dies, something valuable—a golden bowl, a silver cord —is irreparably crushed, and something useful—a pitcher or a wheel—is unexpectedly destroyed. And the dust returns to the earth and the spirit returns to God.

Where does that leave us who are still alive on this earth? We face a future which consists of "evil" days and certain death! What should we conclude then about old age? It can best be described by the words "Vanity of vanities … all is vanity!"

A Conclusion About the Writing of Books

After saying something about both youth and old age, Solomon inserts what might be thought of as a kind of explanatory epilogue in which he tells his readers something about how the book they have just read came to be—while at the same time saying something about the writing of books in general. Listen to verses 9-12:

> In addition to being a wise man, the Preacher also taught the people knowledge; and he pondered, searched out and arranged many proverbs. The Preacher sought to find delightful words and to write words of truth correctly. The words of wise men are like goads, and masters of these collections are like well-driven nails; they are given by one Shepherd.

But beyond this, my son, be warned: the writing of many books is endless, and excessive devotion to books is wearying to the body.

For any aspiring writer, Solomon offers good advice:

1. Know your aim. Solomon's aim was to teach the people knowledge.
2. Use the right words—in Solomon's terminology, words of truth and "delightful" words and words used correctly.
3. Understand the power of the words you write: they can serve as "goads"—prodding people to do right—and as "well-driven nails"—driving home the point the writer is making. Solomon adds this additional truth: If the words of a book are correct and truthful, their real original source is the "Shepherd"—God Himself.

The implication is that the author wrote Ecclesiastes carefully, choosing the best words, to achieve a particular aim, and he planned for his writings to serve as goads which would prod human beings towards doing what God wanted them to do.

The author goes on to say that the reader needs to be warned about what has been written: for one thing, an excessive number of books have been written, implying that not all are worth reading. For another, a devoted reader can become addicted to books—which is not a good thing. If he spends all his time reading, he will get nothing else done.

What should we conclude about books? It is good both to read and to write them, but there are problems —there are too many of them and one can become addicted to reading them. So: Be careful what you read and how you write.

The Conclusion

Finally, after reaching what might be thought of as three less significant conclusions, the author of Ecclesiastes comes to *the* conclusion in 12:13, 14.

> The conclusion, when all has been heard, is: Fear God and keep his commandments, because this applies to every person. For God will bring every act to judgment, everything which is hidden, whether it is good or evil.

The second part of verse 13 is translated "this is the whole duty of man" in the King James Version (also in the RSV, NRSV, ESV). Other versions translate differently: The NASB (as above) has "this applies to every person;" the NIV has "this is the whole duty of all mankind;" the CEV (Contemporary English Version) reads "this is what life is all about." A commentary says that the original is simply "for this is the whole of man" and says that it is an idiom for "every man," then adds that it means "this applies to every man."[2] In any case, the meaning is clear: Everyone has a responsibility to "fear God and keep His commandments." If the KJV translation is correct, this is the main thing God requires of us all—the "whole duty of man."

What is man's responsibility?

- To fear God—to recognize His sovereignty, to acknowledge His power, to stand in awe of Him, with the result that you worship Him.
- To obey His commandments—whatever they are. If one truly fears God he will obey God.

If someone tells you what to do, and you know he is strong and determined and does not put up with disobedience, you do what he tells you. You do not want to experience the consequences of disobedience! In the same way, if you truly fear God, you will do what He says!

These are not just Old Testament commands. Paul told the Corinthians to perfect holiness "in the fear of God" (2 Cor 7:1). Jesus said that not everyone who called him Lord would enter the kingdom but only those who did the will of God (Matt 7:21; see also Heb 5:8, 9; 2 Thess 1:8,9).

Why must we "fear God and keep His commandments"? Solomon tells us in the next verse: because God "will bring every act to judgment," good or bad, public or private. Solomon says that people will be judged on the basis of what they have done—a doctrine also found in the New Testament (2 Cor 5:10; Rev 20:12; Rom 14:12; Matt 25:31–46).

The conclusion then is: Fear God—respect Him, bow before Him. Obey God—do all that He says. Why? Because God will someday judge you, and you will not get away with anything bad that you have done, because everything—even those things you have tried to hide—will be made known. The results of that judgment will be experienced eternally—a truth hinted at in Ecclesiastes when the wise man says that God "has set eternity in their heart" (3:11).

The Conclusion of the Conclusion

What is life all about then? Is it about working for a living? Trying to get rich? Seeking fame? Trying to gain wisdom by getting more and more education? Seeing how much fun you can have, how much pleasure you can get out of life? No! Life is about spiritual things! Life is about pleasing God! Life is about fearing God and keeping His commandments!

Does that disturb you?

Perhaps it should. In this life, "under the sun," what do most people spend most of their time, most of their lives, doing? What are they most interested in, concerned about? What do they live for? What are you most interested in? Whatever it is, what does Solomon say about it?

Does any of the following describe you?

"I'm going to work hard, work at my job, continue to work, and get good at what I do, and someday I will be the best, and I will succeed." Solomon says concerning your work: "It is vanity and striving after wind."

"My aim is to get rich. For that purpose I will give up a lot of things to make sure I make a lot of money. There is nothing wrong with being rich, is there?" Solomon says concerning your riches: "It is vanity and striving after wind."

"Life is not so serious. I have been put here to have fun! My plan is to get as much pleasure out of life as I can! My only question is: How can I have more fun?"

Solomon says, "Vanity! Striving after wind!"

"Me? I am a performer. I belong on a stage. I am going to become famous as an actor or a musician or a singer. That is my talent and that is what I care about!" Solomon says, "This, too, is vanity and striving after wind."

"Give me power and fame! I was president of my

senior class. I am going to become the head of a company—everyone will call me boss! Maybe I will go into politics! I might become President and be the most powerful person in the world!" God says, "This, too, is vanity and striving after wind!"

"I am not like these other people. I want to be wise. I want to get as much knowledge as I can get. I will get a college degree, maybe a graduate degree, maybe even more than one graduate degree! When I get wisdom and get knowledge, then my life will be fulfilled!" Solomon says, "This is vanity and striving after wind!"

How strange! All the things we strive for, the things that dominate our lives! Our hopes, our dreams, our aspirations! The things we spend our lives doing! The things we make the aim of our existence! All vanity and striving after wind! How disturbing! Yet that is what Solomon says: All of these things, in the long run, after all the facts are considered, thinking about what happens "under the sun," in this life, apart from our spiritual responsibility to obey God, without considering eternity—all these things are "vanity and striving after wind."

Is anything meaningful then? Just one thing: "Fear God and keep His commandments!" Do this and other things then become meaningful because they can be used in the service of God. But why? Why is this alone –this requirement to "fear God and keep His commandments—truly significant "under the sun"?

Because it relates to what happens beyond the sun, beyond this life. It relates to what happens in the after-life—in eternity!

Only one thing will ensure that you have life forevermore: "Fear God and keep His commandments!" We will be held accountable for everything we have done, whether good or bad! Judgment is coming! Eternity follows! Eternal life or eternal punishment!

Maybe that should disturb you.

The question is: Do you fear God? Have you obeyed His commandments? If you have not, nothing else matters much until you do!

Discussion Questions

1. Know what Solomon calls "the conclusion of the matter." If we accept the KJV (and other versions) translation that this is "the whole duty of man," how would we reconcile that idea with the fact that we seem to have—and the Bible seems to give us—other "duties" or responsibilities or things we ought to do? If you were to try to apply this teaching—"fear God and keep His commandments" is the primary purpose of life, the reason for existence—what difference would it make in your life?

2. Does the New Testament teach much the

same thing—namely, that whatever one has to do, it should be done in the context of "fearing God and keeping His commandments"—of putting obedience to God before all else? To answer that, consider the following (paraphrased) passages: "Seek first the kingdom of God. "Present your bodies a living sacrifice." "Love God with all." "Deny yourself and take up your cross and follow me."

3. Discuss what it means to get old. Is Solomon's depiction of old age accurate in your opinion? Do you think old people frequently find "no pleasure" in living? What advice would you give them so that they might enjoy life more?

4. Discuss what it means to be young. Young people should be encouraged by the fact that Solomon encourages them to enjoy life. But they should also take note of the fact that they will be held accountable for what they have done in their youth. Are there other reasons why a young person should take care, not only to enjoy life, but to live a good, law-abiding, righteous life?

5. "Remember your Creator in the days of your youth." Is this a common idea in today's world—that young people should fear God

and follow Him? Even if not, is it a wise idea? Would a young person be better off in every way if he or she obeyed this command? Can you give a reason, or reasons, why?

Endnotes

1. The following explanations are taken, in part, from Michael A. Eaton, *Ecclesiastes*. Tyndale Old Testament Commentaries (Downers Grove, IL: Inter-Varsity Press, 1983), 148–150.

2. Eaton, 156.

Scripture Index

Credits

Also by Coy D. Roper

Exodus. Truth for Today Commentary. Searcy, AR: Resource Publications, 2008.

Numbers. Truth for Today Commentary. Searcy, AR: Resource Publications, 2012.

Minor Prophets, 1. Truth for Today Commentary. Searcy, AR: Resource Publications, 2012.

Minor Prophets, 2: Obadiah, Jonah, Micah, Nahum, Habakkuk, Zephaniah, and Haggai. Truth for Today Commentary. Searcy, AR: Resource Publications, 2013.

Minor Prophets, 3: Zechariah and Malachi; the Intertestamental Period. Truth for Today Commentary. Searcy, AR: Resource Publications, 2013.

Ezra, Nehemiah, and Esther. Truth for Today Commentary. Searcy, AR: Resource Publications, 2015.

Potpourri: A Medley of Poetry and Prose. Abilene, TX: Coy D. Roper, 2016.

Leviticus. Truth for Today Commentary. Searcy, AR: Resource Publication, 2017.

Stories We Told: About Our First Eighty-two Years with Poetic Interludes. Abilene, TX: Coy Roper, 2019.

With David Anguish

Luke 1–9. Truth for Today Commentary. Searcy, AR: Resource Publications, 2021.

Also by Cypress Publications

Always Near: Listening for Lessons from God
by Bill Bagents

The Christian Life: Chapters for Bible Teacher
by Ed Gallagher

Cruciform Christ: 52 Reflections on the Gospel of Mark
by Travis Bookout

Easing Life's Hurts 2nd ed.
by Jack Wilhelm and Bill Bagents

Equipping the Saints: A Practical Study of Ephesians 4:11–16
by Bill Bagents and Cory Collins

The Holy Spirit: A Bible Study Guide
by Jack Wilhelm

Jesus the Christ: Chapters for Bible Teachers
by Ed Gallagher

King of Glory: 52 Reflections on the Gospel of John
by Travis Bookout

Rescue: God and Sin in the Old Testament
by John F. Wakefield

Revisiting Life's Oases: Soul-Soothing Stories
by Bill Bagents

Welcoming God's Word: Reading with Head and Heart
by Bill Bagents

To see full catalog of Heritage Christian University Press and its imprint Cypress Publications, visit www.hcu.edu/publications